Building a Security Operations Center (SOC)

James Relington

DEDICATION

To those who seek knowledge, inspiration, and new perspectives—
may this book be a companion on your journey, a spark for curiosity,
and a reminder that every page turned is a step toward discovery.

AKNOWLEDGEMENTS

I would like to express my deepest gratitude to everyone who contributed to the creation of this book. To my colleagues and mentors, your insights and expertise have been invaluable. A special thank you to my family and friends for their unwavering support and encouragement throughout this journey.

Introduction to Security Operations Centers

A Security Operations Center (SOC) is the nerve center of an organization's cybersecurity efforts, dedicated to detecting, analyzing, responding to, and mitigating threats. In an era where cyberattacks are becoming more frequent and sophisticated, a SOC plays a crucial role in protecting an organization's infrastructure, data, and critical assets. The SOC is not just a technological investment but an operational strategy that integrates people, processes, and technology to safeguard an organization's digital environment. It functions as a centralized hub where security professionals work around the clock to monitor and respond to threats in real time.

The importance of a SOC cannot be overstated, as cyber threats continue to evolve at an alarming rate. Organizations that lack a dedicated security operations team often struggle with slow response times, incomplete visibility into their network activity, and an inability to proactively defend against emerging threats. The primary function of a SOC is to establish a proactive and reactive security posture that minimizes risk and enhances the resilience of an organization's cybersecurity defenses. Without a SOC, many businesses are left vulnerable to attacks that can lead to financial loss, reputational damage, and legal consequences.

A SOC is typically staffed with skilled professionals, including security analysts, incident responders, threat hunters, and engineers who specialize in cybersecurity. These individuals work together to monitor security events, investigate potential incidents, and take appropriate action to mitigate threats before they can cause harm. The SOC operates continuously, ensuring that threats are identified and neutralized as quickly as possible. This 24/7 operation is essential in today's digital landscape, where cybercriminals do not adhere to business hours and often launch attacks during off-peak times to maximize impact.

To effectively monitor and defend an organization, a SOC relies on a variety of security tools and technologies. Security Information and Event Management (SIEM) systems play a central role in aggregating and analyzing logs from multiple sources, providing analysts with real-time insights into potential security threats. Intrusion Detection Systems (IDS), Intrusion Prevention Systems (IPS), Endpoint Detection and Response (EDR), and Threat Intelligence Platforms (TIPs) also contribute to the overall security posture of the organization. These technologies enable the SOC team to detect anomalies, track attack patterns, and prevent malicious activities from escalating into full-blown security incidents.

The role of a SOC extends beyond simply monitoring alerts. One of its key responsibilities is incident response, which involves identifying security breaches, containing threats, eradicating malicious activity, and recovering systems to a secure state. A well-functioning SOC follows predefined incident response playbooks and frameworks to ensure a structured and effective approach to handling cyber incidents.

These processes help minimize downtime, reduce financial losses, and prevent attackers from causing further damage. Additionally, the SOC is responsible for continuous improvement, regularly updating and refining security policies, procedures, and strategies based on lessons learned from past incidents.

Threat intelligence is another crucial component of a SOC's operations. By gathering and analyzing intelligence on emerging threats, SOC analysts can anticipate attacks and proactively strengthen defenses. Threat intelligence feeds provide valuable information about known threat actors, attack techniques, and vulnerabilities that can be exploited. This intelligence-driven approach allows the SOC to stay ahead of cybercriminals by implementing countermeasures before an attack occurs. Effective threat intelligence integration helps organizations detect sophisticated threats that traditional security tools may fail to identify.

Another fundamental aspect of a SOC is collaboration. The team must work closely with IT departments, compliance officers, and business leaders to align security operations with the organization's goals and regulatory requirements. Communication and coordination are critical, as security threats often impact multiple areas of a business. Without proper collaboration, security efforts may become fragmented, leading to gaps in coverage and increased vulnerability to attacks. A SOC must also collaborate with external entities such as government agencies, cybersecurity vendors, and threat intelligence sharing communities to gain deeper insights into emerging threats.

The implementation of automation and artificial intelligence (AI) within a SOC has significantly improved its efficiency and effectiveness. Security automation reduces the burden on analysts by automating repetitive tasks such as log analysis, alert triage, and threat correlation. AI-powered analytics enhance threat detection by identifying patterns and anomalies that may indicate malicious activity. These advancements help SOC teams focus on high-priority threats and reduce the risk of analyst fatigue, which can lead to overlooked incidents. The combination of human expertise and machine intelligence strengthens the SOC's ability to respond to cyber threats swiftly and accurately.

Building a SOC requires a significant investment in personnel, technology, and processes. Organizations must carefully plan the structure of their SOC, taking into account factors such as budget, staffing, and security needs. Some organizations choose to build and operate an in-house SOC, while others opt for managed SOC services provided by third-party vendors. The decision depends on various factors, including the organization's size, industry, regulatory requirements, and overall cybersecurity strategy. Regardless of the model chosen, a SOC must be continuously optimized and updated to remain effective against evolving cyber threats.

One of the challenges faced by SOC teams is the overwhelming volume of security alerts generated daily. Many organizations struggle with alert fatigue, where analysts are bombarded with thousands of alerts, making it difficult to distinguish genuine threats from false positives. To address this challenge, SOCs must implement intelligent filtering mechanisms, prioritize alerts based on risk severity, and fine-tune detection rules to minimize unnecessary noise. An efficient SOC focuses on high-fidelity alerts that require immediate attention, ensuring that critical threats are not buried under a flood of minor security events.

Cyber threats are not limited to external attacks. Insider threats, where employees or contractors misuse their access privileges, pose a significant risk to organizations. A SOC must be equipped to detect and mitigate insider threats by monitoring user behavior, identifying anomalies, and enforcing strict access controls. Behavioral analytics and user entity behavior analytics (UEBA) help SOC teams detect suspicious activities that may indicate potential insider threats. Preventing data breaches caused by insiders requires a combination of technical controls, policy enforcement, and employee awareness programs.

A well-established SOC plays a pivotal role in an organization's overall cybersecurity resilience. By continuously monitoring security events, responding to incidents, and adapting to new threats, the SOC acts as a frontline defense against cyberattacks. Organizations that invest in a robust SOC are better equipped to detect and mitigate threats before they escalate into major security incidents. The effectiveness of a SOC depends on the synergy between skilled personnel, advanced security technologies, and well-defined processes. A proactive approach to security operations ensures that businesses can navigate the evolving threat landscape with confidence and resilience.

The Importance of a SOC in Cybersecurity

A Security Operations Center (SOC) is one of the most critical components of a modern cybersecurity strategy. As cyber threats continue to evolve in both complexity and frequency, organizations must establish a centralized unit dedicated to monitoring, detecting, analyzing, and responding to security incidents. Without a well-functioning SOC, businesses, government agencies, and institutions are left vulnerable to an array of cyber threats that can cause severe financial and reputational damage. The increasing sophistication of cyberattacks, combined with the expanding digital footprint of organizations, makes a SOC indispensable for ensuring continuous protection against malicious activities.

The significance of a SOC lies in its ability to provide real-time monitoring and rapid response capabilities. Cyber threats do not adhere to business hours, and attackers often launch their campaigns during weekends, holidays, or off-peak hours to exploit gaps in security coverage. A SOC operates around the clock, ensuring that security incidents are detected and mitigated before they can escalate into full-scale breaches. The ability to continuously monitor an organization's network, systems, and applications allows the SOC team to identify suspicious activities, track malicious behaviors, and neutralize threats before they cause irreversible harm.

One of the primary reasons a SOC is essential is its role in incident detection and response. Cyberattacks are no longer isolated events but rather persistent threats that require continuous vigilance. Organizations that lack a SOC often struggle with delayed incident response times, allowing attackers to infiltrate their systems and remain undetected for extended periods. A SOC is designed to minimize the dwell time of threats by rapidly identifying security breaches and implementing countermeasures to contain and eradicate malicious actors. The faster a security incident is detected, the lower the impact it will have on an organization's operations, data integrity, and overall security posture.

The SOC plays a crucial role in enhancing an organization's threat intelligence capabilities. By gathering, analyzing, and utilizing threat intelligence, the SOC can anticipate potential attacks and develop proactive defense strategies. Threat intelligence allows SOC analysts to stay informed about emerging threats, tactics used by cybercriminals, and vulnerabilities that may be exploited. By integrating external intelligence feeds with internal security data, a SOC can correlate patterns and identify threats that may otherwise go unnoticed. This intelligence-driven approach enables organizations to take preemptive action, strengthening their cybersecurity defenses before an attack occurs.

Another key aspect of a SOC's importance is its ability to enforce compliance and regulatory requirements. Many industries are subject to strict cybersecurity regulations that mandate continuous monitoring, incident reporting, and data protection measures. Organizations that fail to comply with these regulations may face hefty fines, legal consequences, and reputational damage. A SOC helps organizations maintain compliance by implementing security controls, documenting security incidents, and providing audit trails that demonstrate adherence to regulatory frameworks. Whether it is the General Data Protection Regulation (GDPR), the Health Insurance Portability and Accountability Act (HIPAA), or the Payment Card Industry Data Security Standard (PCI DSS), a SOC ensures that an organization meets its cybersecurity obligations.

The expanding attack surface of organizations further highlights the necessity of a SOC. With the rise of cloud computing, remote work, and Internet of Things (IoT) devices, organizations now face an increasingly complex security environment. Traditional security approaches that rely on perimeter defenses are no longer sufficient to protect against modern threats. A SOC provides a centralized and holistic approach to security by continuously monitoring all endpoints, networks, cloud environments, and user activities. This comprehensive visibility enables security teams to detect anomalies, investigate suspicious behavior, and mitigate risks that traditional security tools might overlook.

A SOC is also essential in mitigating insider threats, which are among the most difficult cybersecurity risks to detect and prevent. Employees, contractors, and business partners with access to an organization's systems and data can inadvertently or maliciously cause security incidents. Unlike external threats, insider threats often bypass traditional security measures since they originate from within the organization. A SOC utilizes advanced behavioral analytics to monitor user activities, detect deviations from normal behavior, and identify potential insider threats. By leveraging machine learning and anomaly detection, SOC analysts can differentiate between legitimate user actions and those that indicate malicious intent, preventing data breaches and unauthorized access.

The ability of a SOC to conduct forensic investigations is another critical factor in its importance. When a security incident occurs, organizations must not only contain the threat but also determine how it happened, what data was compromised, and how to prevent similar incidents in the future. A SOC provides forensic capabilities that allow security analysts to reconstruct attack timelines, analyze malicious payloads, and identify vulnerabilities exploited by attackers. These investigations are crucial for strengthening an organization's security posture, improving incident response strategies, and ensuring that lessons learned from previous attacks are applied to future defenses.

The financial impact of cyberattacks further underscores the importance of having a SOC. Data breaches, ransomware attacks, and other security incidents can result in significant financial losses due to downtime, data loss, legal fees, and regulatory fines. Organizations without a SOC often experience prolonged recovery times, increasing the overall cost of a cyber incident. A SOC reduces these financial risks by enabling faster threat detection and response, minimizing the potential damage caused by cyberattacks. By investing in a SOC, organizations can protect their assets, maintain business continuity, and avoid the costly repercussions of security breaches.

As cyber threats continue to evolve, attackers are leveraging increasingly sophisticated techniques to bypass security defenses. A SOC helps organizations stay ahead of these threats by continuously adapting their security strategies, implementing new technologies, and refining their incident response processes. The integration of automation and artificial intelligence within SOC operations enhances efficiency by reducing the time required to analyze and respond to security events. Automated threat detection, machine learning-driven analytics, and security orchestration allow SOC teams to scale their operations and handle large volumes of security data effectively.

A SOC also plays a vital role in building a culture of cybersecurity awareness within an organization. By actively monitoring security threats and sharing insights with other departments, the SOC helps educate employees on best practices, potential risks, and the importance of adhering to security policies. Employees who are aware of cybersecurity risks are less likely to fall victim to phishing attacks, social engineering tactics, or other forms of cyber exploitation. The presence of a SOC reinforces the organization's commitment to cybersecurity, fostering a security-conscious workforce that contributes to overall risk reduction.

The cybersecurity landscape is constantly shifting, with new threats emerging every day. Organizations that lack a dedicated security team often struggle to keep up with these evolving risks, leaving them vulnerable to attacks. A SOC provides the expertise, technology, and processes necessary to protect against modern cyber threats. By continuously monitoring security events, analyzing threats, and responding to incidents, a SOC ensures that organizations can operate securely in an increasingly hostile digital environment. The investment in a SOC is not just about preventing cyberattacks; it is about ensuring the long-term resilience and security of an organization's digital infrastructure.

Defining the Mission and Objectives of a SOC

A Security Operations Center (SOC) serves as the central hub for an organization's cybersecurity operations, ensuring continuous monitoring, detection, response, and mitigation of cyber threats. The mission and objectives of a SOC must be clearly defined to align with the organization's overall security strategy and business goals. Without a well-defined mission, a SOC risks becoming a reactive entity rather than a proactive defender against evolving cyber threats. Establishing a strong mission statement provides the SOC team with a clear purpose, guiding their day-to-day activities and ensuring that their efforts contribute to the overall security posture of the organization.

The primary mission of a SOC is to safeguard an organization's digital assets, infrastructure, and data from cyber threats by maintaining constant vigilance over security events and incidents. This mission encompasses the prevention, detection, investigation, and response to security threats that could compromise the confidentiality, integrity, or availability of critical systems and data. A SOC must operate as a proactive force, not only reacting to threats but also anticipating and mitigating them before they can cause harm. This requires a combination of technology, skilled personnel, and well-defined processes working together in a structured environment.

A key objective of a SOC is to provide real-time security monitoring and threat detection. Cyber threats do not adhere to predictable schedules, and attackers often launch their campaigns during non-business hours to maximize their impact. To counteract this, a SOC must be operational 24/7, continuously monitoring network traffic, system logs, and user activity for any signs of malicious behavior. By leveraging Security Information and Event Management (SIEM) systems, Endpoint Detection and Response (EDR) tools, and advanced analytics, the SOC can rapidly identify anomalies that indicate a potential security incident. The ability to detect threats early is essential for minimizing the damage caused by cyberattacks.

Another critical objective of a SOC is incident response and mitigation. When a security breach occurs, time is of the essence. The SOC must have a structured approach to handling incidents, ensuring that threats are contained before they can spread further. This involves following predefined incident response playbooks that outline the necessary steps to analyze, contain, eradicate, and recover from security incidents. The SOC must coordinate closely with IT teams, legal departments, and executive leadership to ensure a swift and effective response to security breaches. By reducing the time it takes to detect and respond to an attack, the SOC minimizes financial losses, operational disruptions, and reputational damage.

Threat intelligence plays a crucial role in defining the mission of a SOC. One of its objectives is to gather, analyze, and apply threat intelligence to anticipate potential attacks before they occur. Cybercriminals constantly evolve their tactics, techniques, and procedures, making it necessary for SOC analysts to stay ahead of emerging threats. By integrating external intelligence feeds with internal security data, the SOC can enhance its ability to identify adversary tactics and proactively strengthen defenses. Threat intelligence enables the SOC to recognize indicators of compromise, correlate security events, and refine detection mechanisms to address evolving cyber threats.

A SOC must also focus on reducing false positives while maintaining high detection accuracy. Security analysts are often overwhelmed by a massive volume of alerts generated by security tools, many of which turn out to be false alarms. If too many false positives occur, analysts may develop alert fatigue, leading to critical threats being overlooked. The SOC must implement advanced filtering mechanisms, fine-tune detection rules, and utilize machine learning techniques to improve the accuracy of threat detection. By focusing on high-fidelity alerts and refining detection logic, the SOC ensures that analysts can prioritize real threats without being distracted by irrelevant or benign activities.

Ensuring regulatory compliance is another important objective of a SOC. Many organizations are subject to cybersecurity regulations that require continuous monitoring, incident reporting, and adherence to strict security controls. Industries such as finance, healthcare, and government must comply with standards like GDPR, HIPAA, PCI DSS, and ISO 27001. The SOC plays a vital role in maintaining compliance by implementing security policies, monitoring adherence to regulatory requirements, and generating audit reports that demonstrate due diligence in protecting sensitive data. Compliance not only helps organizations avoid legal penalties but also strengthens trust with customers and stakeholders by ensuring data privacy and security.

Another key objective of a SOC is forensic investigation and root cause analysis. When a security incident occurs, it is not enough to simply neutralize the threat; the SOC must determine how the attack happened, what vulnerabilities were exploited, and what measures should be taken to prevent a recurrence. Digital forensics plays a crucial role in this process, allowing SOC analysts to trace attack vectors, analyze malicious payloads, and understand attacker methodologies. A well-functioning SOC conducts detailed post-incident analysis, providing valuable insights that help improve security defenses and refine incident response strategies.

A SOC must also focus on continuous improvement and adaptation. Cyber threats are constantly evolving, and static defense mechanisms are insufficient to counteract modern attack techniques. A SOC must regularly update its security policies, refine detection methodologies, and conduct red team exercises to test its defenses against simulated attacks. By continuously evaluating its effectiveness and identifying areas for improvement, a SOC ensures that it remains a resilient and adaptive security force capable of handling both known and emerging threats. Regular training programs, certifications, and collaboration with industry peers help SOC analysts stay ahead of cyber adversaries.

Collaboration across departments and external partners is another fundamental objective of a SOC. Cybersecurity is not just the responsibility of the security team; it requires coordination with IT, legal, compliance, and executive leadership. The SOC must establish clear communication channels to ensure that security incidents are addressed promptly and that all stakeholders are aware of potential risks. Additionally, collaboration with external threat intelligence communities, law enforcement agencies, and cybersecurity vendors enhances the SOC's ability to detect and respond to threats. Sharing threat intelligence with other organizations strengthens the collective defense against cybercriminals and nation-state actors.

A SOC must also focus on minimizing the overall risk exposure of the organization. This involves proactively identifying and mitigating security vulnerabilities before they can be exploited. Vulnerability management programs, penetration testing, and security audits are essential components of a SOC's operations. By continuously assessing and improving security controls, the SOC helps organizations stay resilient against cyberattacks. Preventive measures such as implementing zero-trust architectures, enforcing least privilege access, and segmenting networks contribute to reducing the attack surface and minimizing potential points of exploitation.

A well-defined SOC mission and objectives provide a strategic foundation for cybersecurity operations. By aligning its goals with the organization's business objectives, regulatory requirements, and risk management strategies, a SOC ensures that it delivers maximum value in protecting digital assets. The combination of real-time monitoring, threat intelligence, incident response, compliance enforcement, forensic analysis, and continuous improvement enables a SOC to function as the cornerstone of an organization's cybersecurity strategy. With a clear mission and well-defined objectives, a SOC becomes not just a defensive entity but an integral part of a proactive and resilient security framework.

Key Functions of a SOC

A Security Operations Center (SOC) is a dedicated facility that plays a crucial role in an organization's cybersecurity strategy. It functions as the central hub for security monitoring, threat detection, incident response, and proactive defense measures. The SOC is responsible for ensuring the protection of an organization's digital assets, networks, and sensitive data by continuously monitoring for security threats, analyzing potential risks, and responding to incidents as they arise. The effectiveness of a SOC depends on its ability to integrate technology, skilled professionals, and well-defined processes to detect, prevent, and mitigate cyber threats before they cause significant damage.

One of the most important functions of a SOC is real-time security monitoring. Cyber threats operate around the clock, and attackers often target organizations during off-peak hours when security teams are less active. A SOC is designed to provide 24/7 monitoring of an organization's entire IT infrastructure, including networks, endpoints, cloud environments, and applications. By continuously collecting and analyzing security logs and event data, the SOC ensures that even the slightest indicators of potential threats are identified as early as possible. This continuous vigilance is essential for minimizing the risk of cyberattacks going undetected for long periods.

Threat detection is another fundamental function of a SOC. Cyber threats are constantly evolving, and attackers employ increasingly sophisticated techniques to bypass traditional security measures. The SOC utilizes a variety of tools, including Security Information and Event Management (SIEM) systems, Intrusion Detection Systems (IDS), and advanced analytics to detect anomalies and suspicious activities. By leveraging machine learning algorithms, behavioral analysis, and correlation techniques, the SOC can distinguish between normal network activity and potential security incidents. Effective threat detection allows organizations to respond quickly before attackers can escalate their activities and cause significant harm.

Incident response is a critical component of SOC operations. When a security breach or cyberattack is detected, the SOC follows a structured process to contain the threat, eradicate malicious activity, and restore affected systems to normal operation. Incident response procedures typically follow industry-standard frameworks, such as the National Institute of Standards and Technology (NIST) guidelines or the SANS Incident Handling Process. The SOC team is trained to analyze attack patterns, identify vulnerabilities exploited by threat actors, and implement remediation measures to prevent similar incidents in the future. A well-executed incident response strategy minimizes downtime, protects sensitive data, and reduces the financial and reputational impact of a security breach.

Threat intelligence gathering and analysis play a vital role in enhancing the capabilities of a SOC. By collecting and analyzing information on emerging cyber threats, attack techniques, and indicators of compromise, the SOC can proactively strengthen an organization's security posture. Threat intelligence sources may include open-source threat feeds, government cybersecurity agencies, industry-specific threat-sharing communities, and proprietary intelligence platforms. The SOC leverages this intelligence to anticipate potential attack vectors, identify adversary tactics, and implement defensive measures before an attack occurs. By staying ahead of cybercriminals, the SOC enhances its ability to detect and prevent advanced threats.

Vulnerability management is another key function of a SOC. Cybercriminals often exploit unpatched software, misconfigured systems, and outdated security controls to gain unauthorized access to an organization's infrastructure. The SOC is responsible for continuously assessing an organization's IT environment for security vulnerabilities and ensuring that they are remediated in a timely manner. This involves conducting regular vulnerability scans, analyzing security patches, and working with IT teams to implement necessary updates. By proactively addressing security weaknesses, the SOC reduces the organization's exposure to cyber threats and enhances overall resilience.

Security automation and orchestration are essential for improving the efficiency of a SOC. The sheer volume of security alerts generated by monitoring tools can overwhelm analysts, leading to alert fatigue and slower response times. To address this challenge, SOCs implement Security Orchestration, Automation, and Response (SOAR) solutions to automate repetitive tasks, streamline workflows, and improve response coordination. Automated incident analysis, alert prioritization, and threat containment measures allow SOC analysts to focus on high-priority threats that require human intervention. The integration of artificial intelligence and machine learning further enhances the SOC's ability to detect and respond to threats more efficiently.

Forensic investigation and root cause analysis are important functions that help SOC teams understand how security incidents occur and what corrective measures are needed. When an organization experiences a cyberattack, it is essential to conduct a thorough investigation to determine the attack vectors, entry points, and techniques used by threat actors. Digital forensics enables SOC analysts to reconstruct attack timelines, analyze malware samples, and extract evidence that may be useful for legal or compliance purposes. A well-executed forensic investigation helps organizations strengthen their defenses by identifying gaps in security controls and preventing similar incidents from recurring.

Compliance management is another critical aspect of SOC operations. Organizations must adhere to industry regulations and security standards, such as the General Data Protection Regulation (GDPR), the Health Insurance Portability and Accountability Act (HIPAA), the Payment Card Industry Data Security Standard (PCI DSS), and the International Organization for Standardization (ISO) security frameworks. The SOC ensures that the organization remains compliant by monitoring security controls, maintaining audit logs, and generating reports for regulatory authorities. By demonstrating adherence to compliance requirements, organizations reduce legal risks, avoid financial penalties, and build trust with customers and stakeholders.

Red teaming and penetration testing are proactive security functions that allow the SOC to test its defenses against real-world attack scenarios. By simulating cyberattacks, SOC teams can evaluate their detection and response capabilities, identify weaknesses in security controls, and fine-tune their incident response strategies. Red teaming exercises involve ethical hackers attempting to breach an organization's security defenses using tactics similar to those employed by real adversaries. The insights gained from these exercises enable the SOC to strengthen its security posture, improve resilience, and stay prepared for emerging threats.

User behavior analytics (UBA) and insider threat detection are essential functions that help the SOC monitor suspicious activities within an organization. Not all threats originate from external attackers; insiders with legitimate access to systems and data can pose significant security risks. The SOC leverages behavioral analytics to establish baselines of normal user activity and detect deviations that may indicate malicious intent. Unusual login patterns, unauthorized data access, and privilege escalations are key indicators that warrant further investigation. By identifying insider threats early, the SOC can prevent data breaches, fraud, and other security violations.

A well-functioning SOC plays a vital role in strengthening an organization's cybersecurity resilience. By integrating continuous monitoring, advanced threat detection, incident response, and proactive defense strategies, the SOC ensures that organizations can effectively mitigate cyber risks. The ability to adapt to evolving threats, leverage intelligence, and enforce compliance requirements makes the SOC an indispensable component of modern cybersecurity operations. A SOC must remain agile, continuously improving its processes, technologies, and skill sets to stay ahead of cybercriminals and protect the organization from emerging security challenges.

SOC Maturity Models and Frameworks

A Security Operations Center (SOC) is an essential component of an organization's cybersecurity strategy, responsible for detecting, analyzing, and responding to cyber threats. However, not all SOCs operate at the same level of efficiency and effectiveness. To measure and improve the capabilities of a SOC, organizations rely on maturity models and frameworks that provide structured guidance for evaluating performance, identifying gaps, and implementing improvements. These models help organizations understand where their SOC stands in terms of capabilities, resources, and technological advancements, allowing them to evolve from basic security monitoring to advanced threat intelligence and proactive defense.

SOC maturity models provide a roadmap for organizations to assess their current cybersecurity operations and determine the steps needed to achieve a more advanced and effective security posture. The maturity of a SOC is typically evaluated based on factors such as the level of automation, the depth of threat intelligence integration, the effectiveness of incident response processes, and the ability to predict and mitigate emerging threats. By following a structured maturity model, organizations can systematically improve their SOC operations, optimize security investments, and enhance their ability to defend against sophisticated cyber threats.

One of the widely recognized SOC maturity models is the Capability Maturity Model (CMM), which defines five levels of maturity ranging from an ad-hoc security operation to a fully optimized and proactive security center. At the lowest level, a SOC operates in a reactive manner with minimal security monitoring and no structured incident response processes. Security operations at this stage are often inconsistent, with little to no documented procedures or automation. As an organization progresses through the maturity levels, it begins to establish formal processes, implement security tools, and enhance its threat detection and response capabilities. At the highest level, a SOC is fully integrated with advanced analytics, automation, and proactive threat-hunting capabilities, allowing it to anticipate and neutralize threats before they escalate into security incidents.

Another important model used to assess SOC maturity is the Gartner SOC Visibility Triad, which focuses on the integration of three key components: Security Information and Event Management (SIEM), Endpoint Detection and Response (EDR), and Network Detection and Response (NDR). This model emphasizes the importance of comprehensive visibility across network traffic, endpoints, and security logs to ensure that organizations can detect and respond to threats effectively. A mature SOC leverages all three components to create a unified security architecture that minimizes blind spots and enhances detection accuracy.

The MITRE ATT&CK framework is another essential tool for measuring and improving SOC maturity. It provides a comprehensive knowledge base of adversary tactics, techniques, and procedures (TTPs) that security teams can use to detect, analyze, and respond to cyber threats. By mapping security incidents to the MITRE ATT&CK framework, SOC analysts can better understand attacker behavior, identify gaps in detection coverage, and refine their security monitoring strategies. Organizations with a high SOC maturity level use the MITRE ATT&CK framework not only for incident response but also for proactive threat hunting, allowing them to detect threats before they cause significant damage.

A mature SOC also aligns its operations with established cybersecurity frameworks such as the National Institute of Standards and Technology (NIST) Cybersecurity Framework. The NIST framework provides a structured approach for organizations to identify, protect, detect, respond to, and recover from cyber threats. By adopting this framework, a SOC ensures that its security practices are aligned with industry standards and best practices. The NIST framework helps organizations assess their security posture, prioritize security investments, and continuously improve their SOC capabilities.

The Cybersecurity Maturity Model Certification (CMMC) is another framework that organizations, particularly those working with government agencies, use to assess the maturity of their cybersecurity operations. CMMC defines five levels of maturity, ranging from basic cyber hygiene practices to advanced security operations that include continuous monitoring, threat intelligence sharing, and proactive defense strategies. Organizations that achieve higher levels of CMMC certification demonstrate a commitment to maintaining strong cybersecurity practices and protecting sensitive data from cyber threats.

SOC maturity models also emphasize the importance of security automation and orchestration. At the early stages of maturity, a SOC relies heavily on manual processes, which can lead to inefficiencies, delayed incident response times, and increased analyst workload. As a SOC matures, it incorporates automation through Security Orchestration, Automation, and Response (SOAR) solutions. These solutions enable the SOC to automate repetitive tasks, streamline incident response workflows, and reduce the time required to detect and mitigate threats. Advanced SOCs leverage artificial intelligence and machine learning to enhance threat detection accuracy and improve overall efficiency.

Threat intelligence integration is another critical factor in SOC maturity. A low-maturity SOC may rely solely on internal security logs and alerts, limiting its ability to detect sophisticated cyber threats. As a SOC matures, it integrates external threat intelligence feeds, collaborates with industry threat-sharing communities, and adopts advanced analytics to predict and prevent attacks. Organizations with a high SOC maturity level use threat intelligence to enhance situational awareness, correlate security events with global threat trends, and proactively strengthen their security defenses.

Incident response and forensic investigation capabilities also improve as a SOC matures. A low-maturity SOC may struggle with slow response times, lack of structured incident response playbooks, and inadequate forensic tools. A mature SOC, on the other hand, has well-documented incident response procedures, advanced forensic analysis capabilities, and a well-trained team of analysts who can quickly contain and remediate security incidents. Regular tabletop exercises, red teaming assessments, and continuous improvement initiatives ensure that the SOC remains prepared to handle emerging cyber threats effectively.

Organizations that invest in SOC maturity models and frameworks benefit from improved security operations, reduced risk exposure, and enhanced resilience against cyber threats. By systematically assessing their SOC capabilities and following a structured roadmap for improvement, organizations can build a security operations center that not only detects and responds to threats but also anticipates and mitigates them before they cause harm. A mature SOC provides comprehensive visibility into security risks, integrates advanced threat intelligence, and leverages automation to improve efficiency, making it a critical component of a strong cybersecurity strategy.

Understanding the Threat Landscape

The modern cybersecurity landscape is constantly evolving, with new threats emerging every day. Organizations must navigate a complex and ever-changing array of cyber risks that range from sophisticated nation-state attacks to financially motivated cybercrime. Understanding the threat landscape is a critical component of an effective security strategy, allowing security teams to anticipate, detect, and mitigate threats before they can cause significant harm. Without a deep understanding of the tactics, techniques, and procedures used by cyber adversaries, organizations are left vulnerable to attacks that can compromise sensitive data, disrupt operations, and damage reputations.

The cyber threat landscape is shaped by a variety of factors, including technological advancements, geopolitical conflicts, and the increasing reliance on digital infrastructure. Attackers continuously refine their methods to exploit vulnerabilities in software, hardware, and human behavior. As organizations adopt cloud computing, mobile devices, and Internet of Things (IoT) technologies, the attack surface expands, providing cybercriminals with more opportunities to launch attacks. Security teams must remain vigilant, continuously updating their knowledge of emerging threats and adapting their defenses accordingly. Threat intelligence plays a crucial role in this effort, enabling security professionals to monitor global cyber threats and anticipate potential risks.

One of the most persistent threats in the cybersecurity landscape is ransomware. Ransomware attacks have become increasingly sophisticated, with attackers using advanced encryption techniques to lock victims out of their systems and demanding payment in cryptocurrency. These attacks often target critical infrastructure, healthcare organizations, and financial institutions, causing widespread disruption and financial losses. Ransomware groups operate as organized criminal enterprises, offering ransomware-as-a-service (RaaS) to less skilled attackers who seek to profit from cyber extortion. Security teams must implement robust backup strategies, endpoint detection and response solutions, and user training programs to mitigate the risk of ransomware infections.

Phishing attacks remain one of the most effective methods for cybercriminals to gain unauthorized access to sensitive information. Attackers use deceptive emails, social engineering tactics, and fraudulent websites to trick users into revealing login credentials, financial information, or other confidential data. Business Email Compromise (BEC) scams, in which attackers impersonate executives or business partners to request fraudulent transactions, have resulted in billions of dollars in financial losses. Security awareness training and advanced email filtering technologies are essential for reducing the success rate of phishing attacks. Organizations must also implement multi-factor authentication (MFA) to add an extra layer of protection against credential theft.

Nation-state actors represent some of the most advanced and persistent cyber threats. These groups, often backed by government agencies, conduct cyber espionage, disrupt critical infrastructure, and influence political events through cyber operations. Nation-state hackers employ sophisticated attack techniques, including zero-day exploits, supply chain compromises, and targeted spear-phishing campaigns. Unlike financially motivated cybercriminals, nation-state actors have access to extensive resources and operate with long-term strategic objectives. Organizations that handle sensitive government data, intellectual property, or critical infrastructure must adopt advanced security measures, including network segmentation, endpoint monitoring, and threat hunting, to defend against state-sponsored cyber threats.

The rise of artificial intelligence (AI) and machine learning (ML) has introduced both opportunities and challenges in cybersecurity. While these technologies enable security teams to detect anomalies and automate threat response, cybercriminals also leverage AI to enhance their attacks. AI-powered malware can evade traditional security defenses, and automated phishing campaigns can generate convincing messages at scale. The use of deepfake technology for social engineering attacks poses additional risks, as attackers can manipulate audio and video to impersonate executives or public figures. Security professionals must stay ahead of these emerging threats by integrating AI-driven security solutions while remaining aware of the potential for adversaries to exploit the same technology.

Cloud security has become a major concern as organizations migrate critical workloads to cloud environments. Cloud platforms offer scalability and flexibility, but they also introduce new security risks. Misconfigured cloud storage, weak identity and access controls, and insecure APIs can expose sensitive data to cyber threats. Attackers frequently target cloud environments with credential-stuffing attacks, exploiting weak or reused passwords to gain unauthorized access. Organizations must adopt a zero-trust security model, enforce least privilege access, and continuously monitor cloud activity to detect and mitigate threats in real time. Proper configuration management and identity protection are essential for securing cloud-based assets.

Insider threats pose a unique challenge, as they originate from within an organization rather than from external attackers. Employees, contractors, or business partners with access to sensitive systems can intentionally or unintentionally compromise security. Insider threats can take many forms, including data theft, sabotage, and unauthorized access to confidential information. Unlike external threats, which rely on exploiting technical vulnerabilities, insider threats often bypass traditional security controls. Behavioral analytics and user entity behavior analytics (UEBA) help security teams detect unusual activity that may indicate an insider threat. Organizations must also enforce strict access controls, conduct regular audits, and foster a culture of security awareness to mitigate insider risks.

The Internet of Things (IoT) has introduced new attack vectors, as connected devices become increasingly prevalent in homes, businesses, and industrial settings. Many IoT devices lack robust security features, making them attractive targets for cybercriminals. Attackers can exploit insecure IoT devices to launch distributed denial-of-service (DDoS) attacks, gain unauthorized access to networks, or manipulate critical systems. Industrial control systems (ICS) and operational technology (OT) environments face heightened risks, as cyberattacks on these systems can disrupt essential services such as power grids, water treatment facilities, and transportation networks. Organizations must implement strong authentication measures, network segmentation, and continuous monitoring to protect IoT and OT environments from cyber threats.

Cryptojacking has emerged as a growing threat, as attackers hijack computing resources to mine cryptocurrency without the owner's consent. Unlike ransomware, which demands a payment from victims, cryptojacking operates covertly, consuming system resources and slowing down performance. Attackers deploy malicious scripts that run in the background, often spreading through compromised websites, unsecured cloud environments, or vulnerable software. The financial incentives behind cryptojacking make it an attractive option for cybercriminals seeking a low-risk, high-reward attack strategy. Security teams must monitor system performance, detect unusual CPU usage, and implement endpoint security measures to prevent cryptojacking attempts.

Supply chain attacks have gained prominence as attackers target third-party vendors and service providers to infiltrate larger organizations. These attacks exploit trust relationships between businesses, injecting malicious code or compromising software updates to spread malware to unsuspecting victims. High-profile supply chain attacks have demonstrated the devastating impact of this tactic, affecting thousands of organizations worldwide. Organizations must conduct thorough security assessments of their vendors, enforce strict access controls, and implement continuous monitoring to detect anomalies in third-party software and services. Supply chain security must be an integral part of an organization's risk management strategy to prevent large-scale breaches.

Cybercriminals continue to evolve their tactics, taking advantage of emerging technologies and vulnerabilities to launch increasingly sophisticated attacks. Organizations must remain proactive in understanding the threat landscape, leveraging threat intelligence, and adopting a multi-layered security approach to defend against cyber threats. Continuous monitoring, advanced analytics, and a well-trained security team are essential for staying ahead of adversaries and ensuring the resilience of digital infrastructure. As the cyber threat landscape grows more complex, organizations that invest in threat intelligence and cybersecurity awareness will be better equipped to protect their assets and maintain operational continuity in the face of evolving cyber risks.

Organizational Structure of a SOC

A Security Operations Center (SOC) is a complex entity that requires a well-defined organizational structure to function efficiently. The structure of a SOC determines how security teams coordinate, communicate, and operate to protect an organization's digital assets. The effectiveness of a SOC depends not only on the tools and technologies it uses but also on the way it is organized and managed. An optimal SOC structure ensures that all security functions are aligned with the organization's overall cybersecurity strategy, enabling rapid threat detection, effective incident response, and proactive defense mechanisms.

At the core of a SOC's organizational structure are multiple layers of security personnel, each with distinct responsibilities. The structure typically consists of three levels of analysts, with each level handling different levels of complexity and response. Tier 1 analysts, also known as SOC operators or security monitoring analysts, serve as the frontline of defense. Their primary responsibility is to monitor security alerts, analyze logs, and escalate incidents that require further investigation. They work with Security Information and Event Management (SIEM) systems to correlate data from multiple sources, identifying patterns and anomalies that indicate potential threats. Their role is critical in filtering out false positives and ensuring that only legitimate security incidents are escalated to higher-tier analysts.

Tier 2 analysts, often referred to as incident responders, handle more complex security incidents. When an alert is escalated from Tier 1, these analysts perform deeper investigations, analyzing malware samples, reviewing network traffic, and identifying the tactics, techniques, and procedures (TTPs) used by attackers. Their job is to determine the root cause of security incidents and implement containment strategies to prevent further damage. Incident responders work closely with forensic specialists and IT teams to mitigate security threats and ensure that compromised systems are restored securely.

Tier 3 analysts, commonly known as threat hunters or advanced security analysts, focus on proactive security measures. Rather than waiting for alerts to indicate potential threats, they actively search for hidden threats that may have bypassed automated security controls. Threat hunters use threat intelligence, behavioral analytics, and attack simulations to identify sophisticated adversaries that operate within an organization's network undetected. Their work is crucial for strengthening the SOC's defense capabilities and improving detection methodologies. By identifying emerging attack patterns, they help refine security policies, fine-tune detection rules, and recommend improvements to the overall security infrastructure.

Beyond the three-tiered analyst structure, the SOC also includes a team of security engineers and architects. Security engineers are responsible for designing, deploying, and maintaining security tools, such as firewalls, SIEM solutions, intrusion detection systems (IDS), and endpoint detection and response (EDR) technologies. They ensure that security solutions are configured correctly, optimized for performance, and capable of handling large-scale security events. Security architects, on the other hand, focus on the overall design and strategy of the SOC, ensuring that security operations align with industry best practices, compliance requirements, and business objectives. Their work involves defining security frameworks, selecting appropriate technologies, and developing policies that guide the SOC's operations.

Another critical role within the SOC is the SOC manager, who oversees the entire operation and ensures that security objectives are met. The SOC manager is responsible for resource allocation, team coordination, and incident management. They ensure that security analysts receive ongoing training, that standard operating procedures (SOPs) are followed, and that security incidents are handled efficiently. The SOC manager also acts as the primary point of contact between the SOC and executive leadership, providing reports on security metrics, incident trends, and overall cybersecurity posture. Effective leadership within the SOC is essential for maintaining operational efficiency and ensuring that security teams remain motivated and well-equipped to handle cyber threats.

Threat intelligence analysts play a crucial role in providing SOC teams with actionable intelligence on emerging threats. They gather data from multiple sources, including open-source intelligence (OSINT), dark web monitoring, government agencies, and industry threat-sharing communities. Their goal is to analyze attack trends, identify adversary groups, and predict potential threats that could target the organization. Threat intelligence analysts work closely with SOC teams to enhance detection capabilities, improve threat-hunting efforts, and refine security policies based on real-world attack scenarios.

Incident response coordinators ensure that security incidents are handled according to established protocols. Their role involves documenting incidents, coordinating response efforts across different teams, and ensuring that lessons learned from security events are incorporated into future security strategies. They work with legal teams, compliance officers, and public relations teams to manage the aftermath of security breaches, ensuring that regulatory requirements are met and that stakeholders are properly informed. Effective incident response coordination minimizes downtime, reduces financial losses, and strengthens the organization's ability to recover from cyberattacks.

Compliance and risk management specialists play an essential role in ensuring that the SOC operates within the regulatory framework applicable to the organization. Many industries require strict adherence to data protection laws, such as the General Data Protection Regulation (GDPR), the Health Insurance Portability and Accountability Act (HIPAA), and the Payment Card Industry Data Security Standard (PCI DSS). Compliance specialists ensure that SOC operations align with these standards, conducting regular audits, generating compliance reports, and implementing security controls that meet regulatory requirements. Their work helps organizations avoid legal penalties and build trust with customers and stakeholders.

SOC teams also collaborate with external security entities, including government agencies, cybersecurity vendors, and threat intelligence communities. Engaging with external organizations allows the SOC to stay informed about global cyber threats and receive early warnings about emerging vulnerabilities. Collaboration with law enforcement agencies is particularly important in cases of cybercrime, fraud, or data breaches that require legal action. SOC teams may also participate in information-sharing initiatives, where they exchange threat intelligence with other organizations in the same industry to collectively improve security defenses.

The organizational structure of a SOC must be flexible and scalable to adapt to the changing cybersecurity landscape. As threats evolve, the SOC must continuously refine its processes, integrate new technologies, and expand its capabilities to address emerging risks. A well-structured SOC is not only reactive but also proactive, actively seeking out threats and mitigating risks before they can impact business operations. A strong SOC requires a combination of skilled professionals, advanced security tools, and a well-defined operational framework to effectively protect the organization from cyber threats. The ability to coordinate different teams, streamline communication, and enforce security policies ensures that the SOC functions as a cohesive unit, capable of defending against even the most sophisticated cyber adversaries.

Roles and Responsibilities in a SOC

A Security Operations Center (SOC) functions as the frontline defense against cyber threats, requiring a well-structured team with clearly defined roles and responsibilities. The effectiveness of a SOC depends on the expertise of its personnel, their ability to work collaboratively, and their adherence to established security protocols. Each team member plays a crucial role in maintaining the security posture of an organization, ensuring rapid detection, analysis, response, and mitigation of cyber incidents. A well-organized SOC operates with a hierarchy of roles, each specializing in different aspects of cybersecurity, incident management, and threat mitigation.

At the foundation of the SOC are the Tier 1 analysts, often referred to as security monitoring analysts or SOC operators. These professionals are responsible for monitoring security alerts, analyzing logs, and identifying potential security incidents. They act as the first line of defense, reviewing automated alerts generated by Security Information and Event Management (SIEM) systems, Intrusion Detection Systems (IDS), and Endpoint Detection and Response (EDR) tools. Their primary responsibility is to triage alerts, distinguishing between false positives and legitimate security threats. If an alert is deemed serious, Tier 1 analysts escalate it to higher-level analysts for further investigation. Their ability to quickly assess threats and filter out irrelevant alerts is crucial in maintaining the efficiency of the SOC.

Tier 2 analysts, also known as incident responders, take over when a security incident requires further investigation. They conduct in-depth analysis of security breaches, assess the scope of an attack, and determine the potential impact on the organization. Their responsibilities include investigating network traffic, analyzing malware samples, and reviewing forensic data to understand how an attack occurred. They also work on containing active threats, preventing further escalation, and implementing immediate countermeasures to minimize damage. Incident responders collaborate closely with IT teams to restore affected systems and ensure that proper security patches and mitigations are applied to prevent similar attacks in the future.

At the top of the analytical hierarchy are Tier 3 analysts, commonly referred to as threat hunters or advanced security analysts. These experts specialize in proactive threat detection, hunting for hidden adversaries that may have bypassed automated security controls. Instead of relying solely on alerts, they analyze patterns, behaviors, and anomalies within the organization's network to identify stealthy attacks. They use threat intelligence feeds, behavioral analytics, and machine learning tools to detect sophisticated cyber threats that traditional security measures might miss. Threat hunters play a critical role in improving detection capabilities, fine-tuning security tools, and developing new strategies to counter evolving attack techniques.

Security engineers and architects form another essential part of the SOC, focusing on designing, deploying, and maintaining security infrastructure. Security engineers ensure that the SOC has the necessary tools and technologies to monitor and defend against threats effectively. They configure and manage firewalls, SIEM platforms, endpoint security solutions, and intrusion prevention systems. Their role includes optimizing security configurations, ensuring compliance with best practices, and automating security processes to improve operational efficiency. Security architects, on the other hand, take a broader strategic approach, designing the overall security framework of the organization. They define security policies, select appropriate technologies, and ensure that security solutions align with business objectives.

The SOC manager oversees the entire security operation, ensuring that all processes run smoothly and that security teams operate effectively. The SOC manager is responsible for staffing, training, resource allocation, and maintaining incident response readiness. They act as the primary liaison between the SOC and senior leadership, providing reports on security metrics, threat trends, and overall cybersecurity posture. The SOC manager plays a vital role in establishing incident response protocols, ensuring compliance with regulatory requirements, and driving continuous improvement initiatives within the SOC. Their leadership ensures that the SOC remains agile and capable of addressing emerging cyber threats.

Threat intelligence analysts play a crucial role in enhancing the SOC's ability to predict and prevent attacks. They gather and analyze intelligence from multiple sources, including dark web forums, industry threat-sharing communities, and government agencies. Their job is to track the activities of cybercriminal groups, identify emerging threats, and provide actionable insights that can help SOC teams strengthen their defenses. Threat intelligence analysts work closely with security analysts and engineers to refine detection rules, develop new threat-hunting techniques, and anticipate the tactics used by adversaries. Their contributions help the SOC stay ahead of evolving cyber threats by leveraging intelligence-driven security measures.

Incident response coordinators ensure that security incidents are handled in a structured and efficient manner. They are responsible for documenting security events, coordinating response efforts across different teams, and ensuring that lessons learned from past incidents are incorporated into future security strategies. Their role involves working with legal teams, compliance officers, and public relations teams to manage the impact of security breaches. They ensure that regulatory requirements are met, that affected stakeholders are informed, and that the organization's reputation is protected. Effective incident response coordination minimizes downtime and ensures a well-organized approach to crisis management.

Compliance and risk management specialists are essential in ensuring that the SOC operates within the boundaries of industry regulations and cybersecurity standards. Many organizations must comply with strict data protection laws such as the General Data Protection Regulation (GDPR), the Health Insurance Portability and Accountability Act (HIPAA), and the Payment Card Industry Data Security Standard (PCI DSS). Compliance specialists ensure that the SOC adheres to these standards by conducting security audits, generating compliance reports, and implementing necessary security controls. Their work helps organizations avoid legal penalties and strengthens overall trust in their cybersecurity practices.

Red team specialists and penetration testers contribute to the SOC by simulating real-world cyberattacks to test the organization's security defenses. These ethical hackers attempt to breach systems using the same techniques employed by malicious adversaries, helping SOC teams identify vulnerabilities before they can be exploited by real attackers. Red team exercises provide valuable insights into weaknesses in security controls, employee awareness, and incident response readiness. By continuously testing and improving defenses, red team specialists help organizations maintain a resilient security posture against cyber threats.

User behavior analytics (UBA) specialists focus on detecting insider threats and anomalous user activities within an organization. They use behavioral analytics to establish baselines for normal user activity and identify deviations that may indicate a security risk. Suspicious login patterns, unauthorized data access, and unusual privilege escalations are some of the red flags that UBA specialists analyze. Their role is crucial in preventing data breaches caused by malicious insiders or compromised user accounts. By monitoring user behavior and enforcing strict access controls, they help the SOC detect and mitigate potential insider threats before they cause significant damage.

The effectiveness of a SOC depends on the collaboration and expertise of its personnel. Each role within the SOC contributes to the overall mission of detecting, responding to, and preventing cyber threats. A well-structured SOC ensures that security teams operate efficiently, that security tools are optimized, and that emerging threats are addressed proactively. By clearly defining roles and responsibilities, organizations can build a SOC that is capable of handling the challenges of an increasingly complex cybersecurity landscape.

Essential Skills for SOC Analysts

A Security Operations Center (SOC) analyst plays a crucial role in defending an organization's digital assets against cyber threats. SOC analysts are responsible for monitoring security alerts, analyzing suspicious activities, and responding to incidents in real time. The effectiveness of a SOC depends on the skills and expertise of its analysts, who must be equipped with a combination of technical, analytical, and soft skills. In an increasingly complex cybersecurity landscape, SOC analysts must possess a broad set of competencies to detect, investigate, and mitigate threats efficiently.

One of the most important skills for SOC analysts is a deep understanding of networking concepts and protocols. Cyberattacks often target network infrastructure, and analysts must be able to interpret network traffic, identify anomalies, and detect unauthorized activities. Knowledge of protocols such as TCP/IP, HTTP, DNS, FTP, and SMTP is essential for identifying attack patterns and tracing malicious activities. Analysts should also be proficient in analyzing network logs and packet captures to understand how data flows within an organization's environment. The ability to detect suspicious connections, lateral movement, and data exfiltration attempts is critical in preventing security breaches.

Proficiency in operating systems, particularly Windows, Linux, and macOS, is another fundamental skill for SOC analysts. Many cyber threats target vulnerabilities within operating systems, and analysts must be able to recognize indicators of compromise at the system level. Understanding system logs, registry modifications, file system changes, and process executions helps analysts identify potential malware infections and unauthorized access. Familiarity with command-line tools such as PowerShell, Bash, and Windows Command Prompt allows analysts to investigate incidents, retrieve forensic evidence, and execute security tasks efficiently. A strong grasp of system administration principles enables analysts to detect misconfigurations and secure endpoints against attacks.

SOC analysts must also have expertise in security tools and technologies, as these are essential for monitoring and responding to threats. Security Information and Event Management (SIEM) systems play a central role in SOC operations, aggregating logs from multiple sources and providing real-time alerts on potential security incidents. Analysts must be proficient in configuring, querying, and analyzing data within SIEM platforms to correlate security events and detect anomalies. Additionally, knowledge of intrusion detection and prevention systems (IDS/IPS), endpoint detection and response (EDR) solutions, and threat intelligence platforms helps analysts enhance their threat detection capabilities. The ability to integrate security tools and automate repetitive tasks improves efficiency and reduces response times.

A strong understanding of malware analysis and threat intelligence is essential for identifying and mitigating advanced cyber threats. SOC analysts must be able to analyze malware behavior, extract indicators of compromise (IOCs), and assess the impact of security incidents. Knowledge of sandboxing techniques, reverse engineering fundamentals, and static and dynamic malware analysis tools helps analysts dissect malicious files and determine their objectives. Threat intelligence skills enable analysts to track emerging attack trends, understand adversary tactics, and apply intelligence-driven defense strategies. The ability to correlate threat intelligence with security incidents enhances the SOC's ability to proactively defend against sophisticated attacks.

Incident response skills are critical for SOC analysts, as they are responsible for handling security breaches and minimizing damage. Analysts must be able to follow structured incident response procedures, including identification, containment, eradication, and recovery. They must document security incidents, communicate findings with relevant stakeholders, and ensure that appropriate mitigation measures are implemented. Understanding forensic investigation techniques allows analysts to reconstruct attack timelines, analyze log data, and determine the root cause of incidents. The ability to conduct memory forensics, analyze disk images, and extract evidence from compromised systems strengthens an organization's ability to respond to and learn from security breaches.

SOC analysts must possess a high level of analytical and problem-solving skills to interpret complex security data and identify meaningful patterns. Cyber threats often involve subtle indicators that may not be immediately obvious, requiring analysts to think critically and connect disparate pieces of information. The ability to perform deep-dive investigations, recognize attack signatures, and differentiate between legitimate activity and malicious behavior is essential. Analysts must be able to assess risks, prioritize security incidents, and make informed decisions under pressure. Strong analytical skills enable SOC analysts to anticipate attack scenarios and implement proactive security measures to reduce organizational risk.

Effective communication skills are also necessary for SOC analysts, as they must collaborate with IT teams, security engineers, management, and external stakeholders. Analysts must be able to convey technical findings in a clear and concise manner, ensuring that non-technical personnel understand the impact of security incidents. Writing detailed incident reports, documenting security events, and providing recommendations for mitigating risks are essential aspects of an analyst's role. Strong communication skills also facilitate teamwork within the SOC, allowing analysts to share knowledge, escalate incidents appropriately, and contribute to continuous security improvements.

SOC analysts must be highly adaptable and continuously willing to learn, as the cybersecurity landscape is constantly evolving. Attackers frequently develop new techniques, and analysts must stay updated on the latest threat intelligence, vulnerabilities, and security best practices. Continuous learning through certifications, cybersecurity training programs, and hands-on labs is essential for maintaining expertise in the field. Industry-recognized certifications such as Certified SOC Analyst (CSA), Certified Information Systems Security

Professional (CISSP), GIAC Security Essentials (GSEC), and Offensive Security Certified Professional (OSCP) help analysts validate their skills and expand their knowledge. The ability to adapt to new security challenges and emerging technologies ensures that SOC analysts remain effective in defending against cyber threats.

Time management and the ability to work under pressure are crucial skills for SOC analysts, as security incidents often require rapid response and resolution. Analysts must be able to manage multiple security alerts simultaneously, prioritize critical threats, and maintain composure during high-pressure situations. Cyberattacks can escalate quickly, requiring analysts to think and act decisively to prevent further damage. The ability to remain focused, organized, and efficient in fast-paced environments ensures that security incidents are handled with precision and urgency.

A strong ethical mindset and a sense of responsibility are essential qualities for SOC analysts. They have access to sensitive data and must adhere to strict ethical standards to ensure confidentiality and integrity. Analysts must follow organizational security policies, respect privacy regulations, and act in the best interest of the organization. Ethical decision-making is critical when handling security incidents, reporting vulnerabilities, and preventing unauthorized data access. A commitment to maintaining high ethical standards reinforces trust within the organization and strengthens the overall security culture.

SOC analysts play a fundamental role in protecting organizations from cyber threats, requiring a diverse skill set that combines technical expertise, analytical thinking, and effective communication. Their ability to detect, analyze, and respond to security incidents directly impacts an organization's ability to defend against cyberattacks. Continuous learning, adaptability, and collaboration are key attributes that enable SOC analysts to stay ahead of emerging threats and contribute to a resilient cybersecurity posture. A well-trained and highly skilled SOC team enhances an organization's ability to mitigate risks, respond to security incidents, and maintain a strong defense against evolving cyber threats.

SOC Budgeting and Resource Allocation

Building and maintaining a Security Operations Center (SOC) requires strategic budgeting and resource allocation to ensure its efficiency and effectiveness. A SOC is a critical investment for an organization, providing continuous monitoring, threat detection, incident response, and risk mitigation. However, due to the increasing complexity of cyber threats and evolving security requirements, organizations must allocate resources wisely to maximize the return on investment while ensuring that the SOC remains fully operational and resilient against cyberattacks. Effective budgeting and resource planning are necessary to strike a balance between security needs, operational efficiency, and financial constraints.

One of the key aspects of SOC budgeting is determining the overall cost structure, which includes personnel, technology, training, and infrastructure. Personnel expenses typically account for the largest portion of a SOC's budget, as skilled cybersecurity professionals are in high demand and command competitive salaries. Hiring and retaining SOC analysts, security engineers, threat intelligence analysts, and incident response specialists require a substantial financial commitment. In addition to salaries, organizations must budget for employee benefits, overtime pay for 24/7 operations, and recruitment costs to attract top-tier talent. Investing in well-trained and experienced professionals is crucial for maintaining an effective SOC, as a shortage of skilled staff can lead to inefficiencies in threat detection and response.

Technology expenditures form another major component of SOC budgeting. Organizations must invest in advanced security tools, including Security Information and Event Management (SIEM) systems, Endpoint Detection and Response (EDR) solutions, Intrusion Detection Systems (IDS), Intrusion Prevention Systems (IPS), and Security Orchestration, Automation, and Response (SOAR) platforms. These technologies enable SOC teams to analyze vast amounts of security data, detect anomalies, and automate response actions. However, acquiring and maintaining these tools can be expensive, requiring careful selection to ensure that investments align with the organization's security needs and budgetary constraints. Organizations must also consider the cost of software licensing, cloud-based security solutions, and third-party threat intelligence services when planning their SOC budget.

Training and continuous education are critical investments in SOC resource allocation. Cyber threats constantly evolve, and SOC personnel must stay updated on the latest attack techniques, security tools, and industry best practices. Organizations must allocate funds for certifications, specialized cybersecurity training programs, and hands-on workshops that enhance the skills of SOC analysts and engineers. Certifications such as Certified Information Systems Security Professional (CISSP), Certified Ethical Hacker (CEH), GIAC Certified Incident Handler (GCIH), and Offensive Security Certified Professional (OSCP) are valuable credentials that enhance the expertise of SOC personnel. Providing ongoing training opportunities not only improves the SOC's capabilities but also helps retain talented professionals who seek career development.

Infrastructure costs are another important consideration in SOC budgeting. Organizations must decide whether to operate an on-premises SOC, leverage a cloud-based SOC, or adopt a hybrid model. An on-premises SOC requires significant investments in physical security, data storage, networking equipment, and backup power solutions. Cloud-based SOCs, on the other hand, offer scalability and cost efficiency by reducing the need for extensive physical infrastructure. However, cloud-based security solutions may come with additional subscription fees and data transfer costs. Hybrid SOC models provide a balance between on-premises and cloud capabilities, allowing organizations to optimize security operations while managing infrastructure costs effectively.

SOC resource allocation must also account for incident response and disaster recovery planning. Cyber incidents can be costly, and organizations must set aside funds for forensic investigations, legal support, and public relations management in the event of a data breach. Having a well-funded incident response plan ensures that the SOC can quickly contain security incidents, minimize damage, and recover critical systems. Organizations should also allocate resources for tabletop exercises, penetration testing, and red team assessments to evaluate the effectiveness of their security controls and response strategies. Regular testing and refinement of incident response procedures help improve SOC readiness and reduce the financial impact of security breaches.

Third-party services and outsourcing options play a role in SOC budgeting and resource allocation. Some organizations choose to partner with Managed Security Service Providers (MSSPs) or Managed Detection and Response (MDR) providers to supplement their SOC capabilities. Outsourcing security operations can reduce the cost of hiring in-house analysts and provide access to specialized expertise. However, relying on third-party services requires careful vendor selection, contract negotiations, and integration with internal security processes. Organizations must evaluate the cost-effectiveness of outsourcing versus maintaining an internal SOC, considering factors such as response times, data privacy requirements, and service-level agreements (SLAs).

Cost optimization is a key factor in SOC budgeting, as organizations must maximize security effectiveness while controlling expenses. Implementing automation and artificial intelligence (AI)-driven security solutions can reduce the burden on analysts, streamline security workflows, and improve incident response efficiency. Automating repetitive tasks such as log analysis, threat correlation, and alert triage reduces operational costs and allows analysts to focus on high-priority threats. Organizations should also conduct cost-benefit analyses to assess the value of security investments and prioritize spending on technologies and initiatives that provide the greatest risk reduction.

Measuring SOC performance through key performance indicators (KPIs) helps justify budget allocations and ensures that resources are being used effectively. Metrics such as mean time to detect (MTTD), mean time to respond (MTTR), false positive rates, and threat intelligence effectiveness provide insights into the SOC's operational efficiency. By continuously monitoring these metrics, organizations can identify areas for improvement, reallocate resources as needed, and optimize their security investments. Reporting SOC performance to executive leadership helps secure ongoing funding and demonstrates the value of cybersecurity initiatives in protecting business operations.

Regulatory compliance and governance also influence SOC budgeting and resource allocation. Many industries are subject to cybersecurity regulations that mandate specific security controls, data protection measures, and incident reporting requirements. Organizations must allocate resources to ensure compliance with standards such as the General Data Protection Regulation (GDPR), the Health Insurance Portability and Accountability Act (HIPAA), the Payment Card Industry Data Security Standard (PCI DSS), and the National Institute of Standards and Technology (NIST) Cybersecurity Framework. Compliance-related expenses may include security audits, risk assessments, policy development, and legal consultations. Investing in compliance not only helps organizations avoid regulatory penalties but also strengthens overall cybersecurity posture.

Scalability and future-proofing are essential considerations in SOC budgeting. As organizations grow and expand their digital infrastructure, the SOC must scale accordingly to accommodate increased security demands. Budgeting for future technology upgrades, additional personnel, and expanding security capabilities ensures that the SOC remains effective as new threats emerge. Organizations should consider adopting flexible budgeting models that allow for adjustments based on evolving cybersecurity risks, business growth, and technological advancements.

A well-planned SOC budget and resource allocation strategy enable organizations to maintain robust security operations while managing costs effectively. By prioritizing personnel, technology investments, training, incident response preparedness, and compliance, organizations can build a resilient SOC capable of defending against advanced cyber threats. Aligning SOC budgeting with business objectives ensures that security investments provide tangible benefits, reduce risk exposure, and enhance overall cybersecurity resilience.

Choosing the Right SOC Model (In-House, Outsourced, Hybrid)

Building a Security Operations Center (SOC) requires organizations to carefully consider which model best aligns with their business needs, security requirements, and budget. Choosing the right SOC model is a crucial decision that impacts the effectiveness of an organization's cybersecurity strategy. The three primary SOC models include in-house, outsourced, and hybrid approaches, each with distinct advantages and challenges. The decision on which model to adopt depends on factors such as the size of the organization, the complexity of its IT infrastructure, regulatory compliance obligations, and the level of control it wants over security operations.

An in-house SOC is fully managed and operated by the organization, providing complete control over security operations, data privacy, and incident response strategies. Organizations that choose an in-house SOC invest in their own security infrastructure, tools, personnel, and processes. One of the main advantages of an in-house SOC is the ability to tailor security operations to the organization's specific needs. Since the SOC is built internally, it can be customized to align with the company's security policies, industry regulations, and risk tolerance. Organizations with high-security requirements, such as financial institutions, government agencies, and healthcare providers, often prefer an in-house SOC because it ensures strict data confidentiality and compliance with regulatory standards.

Operating an in-house SOC requires a significant investment in technology, skilled personnel, and ongoing maintenance. The organization must procure security tools such as Security Information and Event Management (SIEM) systems, Endpoint Detection and Response (EDR) solutions, and Intrusion Detection and Prevention Systems (IDS/IPS). Maintaining a 24/7 security operation also means hiring SOC analysts, security engineers, and threat intelligence specialists. The cost of recruiting, training, and retaining highly skilled cybersecurity professionals can be a challenge, especially given the global shortage of qualified security analysts. Organizations must also ensure that their SOC teams stay updated on the latest cybersecurity threats and trends by investing in continuous education and certifications.

While an in-house SOC offers strong security controls and customization, it also presents scalability challenges. As cyber threats evolve, security operations must adapt quickly, requiring additional investments in technology upgrades and staff expansion. Organizations that lack the resources to maintain a fully operational in-house SOC may struggle to keep up with advanced cyber threats. Small and mid-sized businesses may find that running an in-house SOC is not financially viable due to the high costs associated with infrastructure, staffing, and ongoing improvements.

An outsourced SOC, also known as a managed SOC, is operated by a third-party provider that handles security monitoring, threat detection, and incident response on behalf of the organization. Managed Security Service Providers (MSSPs) and Managed Detection and Response (MDR) providers offer outsourced SOC services, allowing organizations to leverage external expertise and advanced security capabilities without the need for a fully staffed internal security team. One of the key benefits of an outsourced SOC is cost efficiency. Organizations can reduce capital expenditures by eliminating the need to invest in expensive security tools and infrastructure. Instead, they pay a subscription-based fee for security services, making it a more predictable and scalable expense.

Outsourced SOCs provide access to highly experienced security professionals who specialize in threat detection and response. These providers often have global visibility into emerging cyber threats, allowing them to detect and respond to security incidents more effectively. Additionally, outsourced SOCs typically use advanced security technologies, automation, and threat intelligence feeds that may be difficult for organizations to implement on their own. By outsourcing security operations, organizations can focus on their core business activities while benefiting from continuous cybersecurity monitoring and protection.

Despite its advantages, outsourcing a SOC also has limitations. One of the main concerns is reduced control over security operations and incident response. Since an outsourced SOC is managed by a third party, organizations may have limited visibility into security incidents and may not be able to customize security policies according to their specific needs. Response times may also vary depending on the service-level agreement (SLA) established with the provider. Some organizations may find it challenging to coordinate with an external SOC, especially during critical security incidents that require immediate action.

Data privacy and compliance are additional concerns when outsourcing a SOC. Organizations that handle sensitive or regulated data must ensure that their outsourced security provider complies with industry regulations such as the General Data Protection Regulation (GDPR), the Health Insurance Portability and Accountability Act (HIPAA), and the Payment Card Industry Data Security Standard (PCI DSS). Working with a third-party provider requires clear contractual agreements that define data handling policies, breach notification procedures, and compliance responsibilities. Without proper governance, organizations may face legal and reputational risks associated with outsourcing security operations.

A hybrid SOC model combines elements of both in-house and outsourced security operations, offering a balance between control, flexibility, and cost efficiency. In a hybrid approach, an organization retains some security functions internally while outsourcing specific tasks to a managed security provider. This model allows organizations to maintain control over critical security operations while leveraging external expertise for specialized functions such as threat intelligence, forensic investigations, or 24/7 monitoring.

One of the main advantages of a hybrid SOC is its ability to enhance security capabilities without the need for a full-scale in-house SOC. Organizations can rely on their internal security team to manage sensitive data, incident response, and compliance requirements while using external security providers for threat detection, log management, and security analytics. This approach reduces the burden on internal teams and enables organizations to benefit from the expertise and scalability of managed security services.

Hybrid SOCs are particularly useful for organizations that have existing security teams but require additional support for certain security operations. For example, an organization may operate an in-house SOC during business hours while outsourcing after-hours security monitoring to an MSSP. This ensures continuous threat detection without the need to hire a full overnight security team. Similarly, organizations that need advanced threat-hunting capabilities but lack the internal expertise can partner with external threat intelligence providers to enhance their security posture.

However, managing a hybrid SOC requires strong coordination between internal and external teams. Organizations must establish clear communication protocols, incident response workflows, and integration points between their in-house security tools and outsourced services. Effective governance and collaboration are essential to ensuring that security incidents are handled efficiently, regardless of whether they are managed internally or by an external provider. Security leaders must also continuously evaluate the performance of both internal teams and third-party providers to ensure that security objectives are met.

Choosing the right SOC model depends on the organization's security requirements, budget, and operational goals. An in-house SOC provides full control and customization but requires significant investment in personnel and technology. An outsourced SOC offers cost efficiency and access to expert security professionals but may have limitations in control and response times. A hybrid SOC combines the strengths of both approaches, providing flexibility and scalability while ensuring critical security functions remain in-house. Organizations must carefully assess their cybersecurity needs, regulatory obligations, and resource availability before selecting the SOC model that best aligns with their risk management strategy.

Designing the SOC Architecture

A well-designed Security Operations Center (SOC) architecture is the foundation of an effective cybersecurity strategy. The architecture of a SOC determines how security tools, personnel, processes, and technologies are integrated to provide continuous threat monitoring, detection, and response. A properly structured SOC enhances an organization's ability to defend against cyber threats while ensuring seamless communication and collaboration between security teams. Designing the SOC architecture requires careful planning, considering factors such as network visibility, scalability, automation, compliance, and integration with existing IT infrastructure. Organizations must strike a balance between security, operational efficiency, and cost to create an optimized SOC that meets their unique security needs.

The first step in designing a SOC architecture is defining its scope and objectives. The SOC must be designed to align with the organization's business requirements, risk tolerance, regulatory compliance obligations, and overall cybersecurity strategy. Some SOCs focus on internal enterprise security, monitoring corporate networks, cloud environments, and endpoints for threats. Others are built for managed security services, monitoring multiple organizations as part of a service provider model. The scope of the SOC dictates the architecture's complexity, the volume of security data that must be processed, and the required level of automation and staffing. Organizations must clearly define the SOC's mission, operational goals, and performance metrics before beginning the architecture design process.

A key component of SOC architecture is data collection and log aggregation. The SOC relies on Security Information and Event Management (SIEM) systems to centralize security event data from various sources. These sources include firewalls, intrusion detection systems (IDS), endpoint security solutions, cloud security platforms, network traffic logs, application logs, and identity and access management (IAM) systems. The SOC architecture must ensure seamless data ingestion from all relevant security sources, enabling analysts to correlate events, detect anomalies, and respond to threats efficiently. Log retention policies must also be defined to comply with regulatory requirements and support forensic investigations.

Network visibility is a critical aspect of SOC architecture, as attackers often exploit blind spots within an organization's infrastructure. A well-designed SOC must incorporate full network traffic monitoring, ensuring that security teams can detect suspicious activity across all network segments. Implementing network detection and response (NDR) solutions allows SOC analysts to analyze network traffic patterns, identify lateral movement, and detect potential exfiltration of sensitive data. Properly segmenting the network ensures that high-value assets are protected, limiting the impact of an attack if a breach occurs.

Endpoint security is another essential consideration when designing a SOC architecture. Endpoints, including workstations, servers, mobile devices, and Internet of Things (IoT) devices, represent common entry points for cyber threats. A SOC must integrate endpoint detection and response (EDR) solutions to continuously monitor endpoint activity, detect malware infections, and block unauthorized access attempts. The architecture should support real-time threat intelligence sharing between endpoint security tools and other SOC components to improve incident detection and response. Implementing strong endpoint security measures reduces the attack surface and enhances the SOC's ability to contain threats before they escalate.

Automation and orchestration play a crucial role in optimizing SOC architecture. As security alerts continue to increase in volume and complexity, SOC teams must leverage automation to enhance efficiency and reduce response times. Security Orchestration, Automation, and Response (SOAR) platforms streamline workflows by automating repetitive tasks such as log analysis, alert triage, and threat correlation. Automated response actions, such as isolating compromised endpoints or blocking malicious IP addresses, enable SOC analysts to focus on high-priority threats rather than spending time on manual investigations. Integrating artificial intelligence and machine learning further improves the SOC's ability to detect sophisticated threats that traditional security tools may overlook.

Threat intelligence integration is a fundamental component of a SOC's architecture. A well-designed SOC must ingest and analyze threat intelligence feeds from multiple sources, including government agencies, industry threat-sharing communities, commercial threat intelligence providers, and open-source intelligence (OSINT). By leveraging real-time threat intelligence, SOC analysts can proactively detect adversary tactics, techniques, and procedures (TTPs) and implement countermeasures before an attack occurs. The SOC architecture must facilitate seamless integration between threat intelligence platforms, SIEM solutions, and endpoint security tools to maximize threat detection capabilities.

Incident response capabilities must be built into the SOC architecture to ensure rapid containment and mitigation of security incidents. The SOC should have a dedicated incident response framework that defines escalation procedures, communication workflows, and forensic analysis capabilities. The architecture should include secure forensic data storage, enabling analysts to conduct deep-dive investigations into cyber incidents. Integration with digital forensics tools enhances the SOC's ability to analyze malware, trace attacker activities, and identify vulnerabilities that need remediation. The SOC must also have predefined playbooks for common attack scenarios, ensuring that security incidents are handled consistently and efficiently.

Compliance and regulatory requirements influence SOC architecture design, as organizations must ensure that security operations adhere to industry standards and legal obligations. SOCs handling sensitive data must comply with regulations such as the General Data Protection Regulation (GDPR), the Health Insurance Portability and Accountability Act (HIPAA), the Payment Card Industry Data Security Standard (PCI DSS), and the National Institute of Standards and Technology (NIST) Cybersecurity Framework. The SOC architecture must include mechanisms for generating compliance reports, auditing security events, and enforcing data protection policies. Organizations must also implement access controls, encryption, and secure log management practices to meet compliance requirements.

Scalability and future-proofing are essential considerations when designing SOC architecture. Cyber threats are constantly evolving, and organizations must ensure that their SOC can adapt to emerging risks and increasing data volumes. The architecture should be flexible enough to accommodate new security technologies, additional data sources, and expanded monitoring capabilities. Cloud-based SOC architectures provide scalability and flexibility, allowing organizations to leverage cloud-native security tools, automate security operations, and scale resources as needed. A hybrid SOC model, which combines on-premises and cloud security solutions, offers a balance between control and scalability, ensuring that security teams can respond effectively to modern cyber threats.

Collaboration and communication tools must be incorporated into the SOC architecture to enable efficient teamwork among analysts, engineers, and external stakeholders. SOC teams must have secure communication channels to coordinate incident response efforts, share threat intelligence, and document security incidents. Security collaboration platforms, integrated ticketing systems, and case management tools improve workflow efficiency and knowledge sharing within the SOC. Additionally, integration with law enforcement agencies, external cybersecurity vendors, and threat intelligence-sharing communities enhances the SOC's ability to respond to large-scale cyber threats.

A well-designed SOC architecture forms the backbone of an organization's cybersecurity defense, enabling security teams to detect, investigate, and mitigate threats effectively. Organizations must invest in the right technologies, optimize workflows, and ensure seamless integration between security tools to build a robust SOC that can withstand the evolving cyber threat landscape. Proper planning, continuous assessment, and adaptability are key to ensuring that the SOC remains resilient, scalable, and capable of defending against modern cyber adversaries.

Selecting the Right Location for Your SOC

Establishing a Security Operations Center (SOC) is a strategic decision that requires careful planning, and one of the most important considerations is selecting the right location. The location of a SOC directly impacts its efficiency, operational resilience, security, and ability to attract skilled personnel. Organizations must evaluate multiple factors when choosing where to set up their SOC, including geographic risks, regulatory requirements, cost implications, accessibility, infrastructure reliability, and the availability of cybersecurity talent. A well-chosen location ensures that the SOC operates smoothly, remains protected from potential disruptions, and provides an optimal working environment for security professionals.

One of the primary considerations when selecting a SOC location is physical security. A SOC is a highly sensitive facility that handles critical cybersecurity operations, making it a prime target for cybercriminals, insider threats, and even physical intrusions. The chosen site must be in a secure area, away from high-crime zones, and equipped with multiple layers of physical security. Secure access control mechanisms such as biometric authentication, keycard entry systems, and surveillance cameras should be implemented to restrict unauthorized access. Security personnel should monitor the facility around the clock, and all visitors should be logged and verified before entering the premises.

Geopolitical stability is another key factor that influences SOC location selection. Organizations operating in politically unstable regions face increased risks of government-imposed restrictions, internet censorship, and potential cyber warfare activities. If a SOC is located in a country with uncertain political or economic conditions, its ability to function effectively could be compromised. For multinational organizations, establishing a SOC in a geopolitically stable country reduces the risk of government interference, service disruptions, or cyber threats originating from hostile nation-states. Organizations must assess the long-term stability of a location before committing to building a SOC in that region.

Regulatory compliance and legal considerations also play a crucial role in selecting a SOC location. Many industries and governments impose strict regulations on how security operations are conducted, especially when it comes to handling sensitive data. Depending on the country or region, data sovereignty laws may require that specific types of data be stored and processed within national borders. Organizations operating in highly regulated industries such as finance, healthcare, and government services must ensure that their SOC complies with frameworks such as GDPR, HIPAA, PCI DSS, and other local regulations. Choosing a location that aligns with legal and compliance requirements helps prevent legal complications and costly fines.

Proximity to skilled cybersecurity professionals is essential for staffing and maintaining an effective SOC. A SOC requires a team of highly trained analysts, engineers, and incident response specialists who possess expertise in threat detection, incident handling, and forensic analysis. Organizations must consider whether the chosen location has access to a strong talent pool with the necessary cybersecurity skills. Establishing a SOC in a region with a thriving cybersecurity industry, well-regarded universities, or government-supported cybersecurity initiatives increases the likelihood of recruiting and retaining top-tier talent. If the local talent pool is limited, organizations may need to invest in training programs, remote work solutions, or incentives to attract skilled professionals.

Connectivity and infrastructure reliability are critical factors in determining SOC location. Since a SOC relies on real-time monitoring, threat intelligence feeds, and incident response coordination, it must have access to high-speed, redundant internet connections with minimal latency. The facility should be connected to multiple internet service providers (ISPs) to ensure continuous operations in case one provider experiences an outage. Additionally, the SOC must have robust power supply infrastructure, including uninterruptible power supply (UPS) systems and backup generators, to protect against power failures. A well-designed SOC facility should also have redundant cooling systems to prevent overheating of critical security equipment.

Disaster recovery and business continuity planning must be considered when selecting a SOC location. The SOC should be located in an area that is not highly susceptible to natural disasters such as earthquakes, floods, hurricanes, or wildfires. If a SOC is established in a region prone to such events, the organization must implement comprehensive disaster recovery plans to ensure that operations can continue even in the event of a crisis. Some organizations choose to establish multiple SOCs in geographically diverse locations to provide redundancy and ensure that operations remain uninterrupted in case of a localized disaster. Cloud-based SOC solutions can also serve as backup in case of physical SOC failure.

Cost considerations significantly impact SOC location selection. The expenses associated with leasing or purchasing office space, hiring personnel, and maintaining security infrastructure vary depending on the region. While large metropolitan areas offer access to top talent and robust infrastructure, they also tend to have higher operational costs. Some organizations opt to establish SOCs in secondary cities or regions with lower costs of living, where they can still access skilled professionals without incurring excessive expenses. A cost-benefit analysis should be conducted to determine whether the financial investment in a particular location aligns with the organization's budget and long-term objectives.

Time zone considerations can influence the efficiency of SOC operations, especially for global organizations that require round-the-clock security monitoring. If an organization operates in multiple time zones, it may choose to establish SOCs in different geographical regions to ensure continuous coverage. This approach, known as a follow-the-sun model, enables security analysts in different locations to handle security incidents as they occur, reducing fatigue and improving overall response times. Organizations must assess whether a single-location SOC can meet their operational needs or if a distributed approach is more suitable for providing 24/7 monitoring without requiring excessive shift work for employees.

Scalability and future growth potential should also be factored into SOC location selection. As cyber threats continue to evolve, organizations must be able to expand their SOC capabilities to keep up with increasing security demands. Selecting a location with room for physical expansion, the ability to integrate new technologies, and access to additional talent ensures that the SOC remains effective in the long term. If an organization plans to scale its security operations, it should choose a location that can accommodate future workforce growth, additional security technologies, and increased monitoring capabilities.

Organizations must also consider whether to establish a dedicated SOC facility or integrate SOC operations within an existing office. A dedicated SOC facility offers maximum security, allowing organizations to control access, optimize the physical environment for cybersecurity operations, and ensure operational independence. However, setting up a standalone SOC requires a significant financial investment. Integrating the SOC within an existing office can reduce costs but may introduce challenges related to security zoning, noise control, and maintaining a controlled work environment. The decision between a dedicated SOC facility and a shared office SOC depends on the organization's security requirements, budget, and operational needs.

Selecting the right SOC location requires a comprehensive evaluation of multiple factors, including security, talent availability, cost, connectivity, regulatory compliance, and resilience to disruptions. A well-chosen location enhances SOC efficiency, ensures access to skilled cybersecurity professionals, and minimizes operational risks. Organizations must carefully assess their specific requirements and strategic objectives before making a final decision on where to establish their SOC, ensuring that the facility supports their long-term cybersecurity goals while maintaining resilience against evolving cyber threats.

Security Information and Event Management (SIEM)

Security Information and Event Management (SIEM) is a foundational technology in modern cybersecurity operations, playing a central role in threat detection, incident response, and compliance management. SIEM systems aggregate, analyze, and correlate security event data from multiple sources to provide real-time visibility into an organization's security posture. By centralizing log collection and applying advanced analytics, SIEM helps security teams identify threats, detect anomalies, and respond to security incidents before they escalate. The effectiveness of a Security Operations Center (SOC) relies heavily on the capabilities of its SIEM system, making it one of the most critical investments for any organization aiming to strengthen its cybersecurity defenses.

A SIEM platform collects security logs and event data from various sources, including firewalls, intrusion detection systems (IDS), antivirus software, endpoint detection and response (EDR) tools, cloud security services, authentication servers, and network devices. These logs provide valuable insights into user activities, network traffic, system events, and potential security threats. By consolidating data from diverse sources, SIEM enables security analysts to gain a comprehensive view of an organization's security environment. Without a SIEM, organizations would struggle to manage and analyze the vast amount of security data generated across their IT infrastructure, making it difficult to detect coordinated attacks or subtle signs of compromise.

One of the primary functions of SIEM is real-time threat detection through event correlation. Traditional security tools generate a large number of alerts, many of which are false positives or low-priority events. SIEM uses advanced correlation rules and machine learning algorithms to analyze security events in context, identifying patterns that indicate potential threats. For example, a failed login attempt on a single account may not raise suspicion, but a series of failed login attempts from multiple IP addresses within a short timeframe may indicate a brute-force attack. SIEM correlates these events and prioritizes them for further investigation, reducing the burden on security analysts and improving response efficiency.

SIEM systems also support compliance reporting and regulatory adherence by maintaining detailed audit logs of security events. Organizations in regulated industries, such as finance, healthcare, and government, must comply with strict cybersecurity standards that require continuous monitoring, incident logging, and timely reporting of security incidents. Compliance frameworks such as the General Data Protection Regulation (GDPR), the Health Insurance Portability and Accountability Act (HIPAA), the Payment Card Industry Data Security Standard (PCI DSS), and the National Institute of Standards and Technology (NIST) Cybersecurity Framework require organizations to track and document security events to ensure data protection and regulatory compliance. SIEM automates compliance reporting by generating logs, audit trails, and reports that demonstrate adherence to security policies and regulatory requirements.

Advanced SIEM platforms leverage artificial intelligence (AI) and machine learning to enhance threat detection and reduce false positives. Traditional SIEM solutions rely on rule-based correlation, which can be effective but may struggle to detect emerging threats that do not match predefined attack patterns. AI-driven SIEM systems analyze historical data, learn normal behavior patterns, and identify deviations that may indicate suspicious activity. By continuously adapting to new threats and attack techniques, machine learning-based SIEM improves the accuracy of threat detection while minimizing noise from false alarms. This capability is especially valuable in modern cybersecurity environments, where attackers frequently modify their tactics to evade traditional detection methods.

The ability to perform forensic investigations is another critical function of SIEM. When a security incident occurs, analysts need to quickly determine the scope of the attack, how the adversary gained access, and what data or systems were compromised. SIEM provides historical event logs that enable forensic analysis, allowing security teams to reconstruct attack timelines, trace malicious activities, and identify vulnerabilities that need remediation. By providing a centralized repository of security data, SIEM facilitates deep investigations and supports legal or regulatory inquiries in the aftermath of a cyber incident. The ability to rapidly access and analyze historical security data is essential for minimizing the impact of security breaches and strengthening future defenses.

Integration with threat intelligence feeds enhances SIEM's ability to detect and prevent cyberattacks. Threat intelligence provides real-time information on known attack signatures, malicious IP addresses, indicators of compromise (IOCs), and adversary tactics, techniques, and procedures (TTPs). SIEM platforms ingest threat intelligence feeds and automatically compare incoming security events against known threat indicators. If a match is found, the system generates alerts and allows security teams to take proactive measures to block malicious activities. By incorporating threat intelligence, SIEM helps organizations stay ahead of evolving threats and detect attacks before they cause significant damage.

Security automation and orchestration capabilities further enhance SIEM effectiveness by streamlining incident response workflows. Traditional security operations often involve manual investigation and response, which can be time-consuming and inefficient. Modern SIEM platforms integrate with Security Orchestration, Automation, and Response (SOAR) solutions to automate repetitive tasks, such as alert triage, threat containment, and remediation actions. For example, if SIEM detects a suspicious login attempt from an unauthorized location, it can automatically trigger an action to block the IP address, disable the compromised account, and notify security personnel. Automation reduces response times, minimizes human error, and allows SOC analysts to focus on more complex security challenges.

Cloud-based SIEM solutions are becoming increasingly popular as organizations migrate workloads to cloud environments. Traditional on-premises SIEM solutions require significant hardware investments and ongoing maintenance, making them costly and difficult to scale. Cloud-native SIEM platforms offer greater flexibility, scalability, and cost efficiency by leveraging cloud computing resources to process and analyze security events in real time. Organizations that operate in multi-cloud environments benefit from cloud-based SIEM, as it provides unified security monitoring across different cloud service providers. Cloud SIEM solutions also facilitate faster deployment, automatic updates, and seamless integration with modern cloud security tools.

Despite its many advantages, implementing and managing a SIEM system comes with challenges. One of the main difficulties is managing the high volume of security data generated by modern IT environments. Organizations must fine-tune SIEM configurations to filter out unnecessary logs, optimize alert thresholds, and reduce noise from false positives. Additionally, SIEM requires skilled security analysts who can interpret alerts, investigate security incidents, and fine-tune detection rules. Without proper training and expertise, organizations may struggle to maximize the value of their SIEM investment. To overcome these challenges, organizations should regularly update SIEM rules, integrate automation, and provide ongoing training for SOC personnel.

Security Information and Event Management is a critical component of modern cybersecurity, providing real-time threat detection, incident response capabilities, forensic investigation tools, and compliance support. By centralizing security event data, correlating threats, and integrating automation, SIEM enhances an organization's ability to detect and mitigate cyber threats effectively. As cyber threats continue to evolve, organizations must continuously refine their SIEM strategies, incorporate threat intelligence, and leverage advanced analytics to stay ahead of attackers. A well-implemented SIEM system strengthens security posture, improves response efficiency, and ensures that organizations remain resilient against sophisticated cyber threats.

Threat Intelligence Integration in a SOC

Threat intelligence integration is a critical component of a modern Security Operations Center (SOC), enhancing its ability to detect, analyze, and respond to cyber threats effectively. In an increasingly complex and evolving threat landscape, organizations must stay ahead of adversaries by leveraging real-time, actionable intelligence to improve security posture. Threat intelligence provides valuable insights into malicious actors, attack methodologies, and indicators of compromise (IOCs), allowing SOC analysts to proactively identify and mitigate threats before they escalate into full-scale security incidents. By integrating threat intelligence into SOC workflows, organizations can improve situational awareness, reduce false positives, and strengthen incident response capabilities.

A well-integrated threat intelligence system enables a SOC to aggregate and analyze information from multiple sources, including open-source intelligence (OSINT), commercial threat intelligence providers, government agencies, industry-specific Information Sharing and Analysis Centers (ISACs), dark web monitoring, and internal security data. By consolidating intelligence from various sources, SOC analysts gain a comprehensive view of the threat landscape and can correlate this data with real-time security events. This integration enhances the SOC's ability to detect known and emerging threats, helping analysts prioritize and respond to security incidents with greater accuracy and efficiency.

One of the key benefits of threat intelligence integration is the ability to identify adversary tactics, techniques, and procedures (TTPs) before they can be exploited against the organization. The MITRE ATT&CK framework is widely used within SOCs to map security incidents to known attack techniques, providing analysts with insights into how threat actors operate. By integrating threat intelligence feeds into the SOC's Security Information and Event Management (SIEM) system, security teams can automatically compare incoming security events against known indicators of compromise. This automated correlation helps detect malicious activities that might otherwise go unnoticed, enabling a faster and more effective response.

Threat intelligence also plays a crucial role in reducing the volume of false positives that SOC analysts must investigate. Traditional security tools generate a high number of alerts, many of which may not be associated with actual threats. Without contextual threat intelligence, SOC analysts may waste valuable time investigating benign or low-priority events. By enriching security alerts with threat intelligence data, SOC teams can determine whether an event is associated with a known malicious campaign, an emerging threat, or simply a routine system activity. This prioritization ensures that analysts focus on the most critical threats, improving overall operational efficiency.

Incorporating threat intelligence into SOC operations enhances proactive defense strategies, such as threat hunting and red teaming exercises. Threat hunters use intelligence data to search for advanced persistent threats (APTs) that may have evaded automated detection mechanisms. By analyzing threat actor behaviors, SOC teams can proactively identify signs of compromise and investigate suspicious activities before they lead to security breaches. Red team exercises, which simulate real-world attacks, benefit from threat intelligence by replicating the tactics used by actual adversaries, allowing SOC teams to refine their detection and response capabilities.

Automation and artificial intelligence (AI) are increasingly being used to streamline threat intelligence integration within SOCs. Security Orchestration, Automation, and Response (SOAR) platforms enable automated ingestion, analysis, and correlation of threat intelligence data, reducing the manual workload for analysts. AI-powered threat intelligence platforms use machine learning algorithms to analyze large volumes of threat data, identify patterns, and predict potential attack vectors. By leveraging automation and AI-driven analytics, SOC teams can process threat intelligence data more efficiently, detect emerging threats in real time, and implement automated response actions to mitigate risks.

Collaboration and information sharing are essential aspects of threat intelligence integration in a SOC. Cyber threats are constantly evolving, and no single organization has complete visibility into the entire threat landscape. By participating in industry threat intelligence sharing programs, organizations can exchange critical security information with peers, government agencies, and cybersecurity vendors. ISACs, for example, facilitate the sharing of threat intelligence among organizations within the same industry, helping SOC teams stay informed about sector-specific threats. Collaboration with law enforcement agencies and international cybersecurity organizations further enhances the ability to track and combat cybercriminal activities.

Threat intelligence integration also improves incident response by providing SOC teams with contextual information about ongoing attacks. When an incident occurs, analysts must quickly determine the scope, severity, and impact of the threat. Threat intelligence data helps analysts understand whether the attack is part of a larger campaign, which threat actors are involved, and what countermeasures have been effective against similar attacks in the past. This intelligence-driven approach enables SOC teams to respond more strategically, implementing targeted mitigation strategies and preventing further damage.

Cyber threat intelligence can be categorized into three main types: strategic, tactical, and operational intelligence. Strategic threat intelligence provides high-level insights into cyber threats, focusing on trends, geopolitical factors, and risk assessments that influence security decision-making. Tactical threat intelligence includes details about adversary tactics and techniques, helping SOC teams refine their detection and mitigation strategies. Operational threat intelligence consists of real-time indicators of compromise, such as IP addresses, domain names, and malware signatures, which can be directly integrated into security tools for automated detection and blocking. A well-structured SOC leverages all three types of threat intelligence to enhance its security operations and improve resilience against cyber threats.

SOC teams must ensure that threat intelligence feeds are relevant, accurate, and up to date. Not all intelligence sources provide actionable data, and outdated or low-quality intelligence can lead to unnecessary alerts and wasted resources. Organizations should validate the credibility of their threat intelligence providers, conduct regular assessments of intelligence accuracy, and establish mechanisms for filtering out irrelevant or redundant information. The effectiveness of threat intelligence integration depends on the ability of SOC teams to process, analyze, and apply intelligence data in a meaningful way.

As cyber threats become more sophisticated, SOCs must continuously evolve their threat intelligence capabilities. The integration of threat intelligence into security monitoring, incident response, and threat-hunting activities strengthens an organization's overall cybersecurity posture. By leveraging real-time intelligence, automation, and collaboration with industry partners, SOCs can enhance their ability to detect and mitigate threats proactively. Investing in robust threat intelligence integration not only improves the efficiency of SOC operations but also enables organizations to stay ahead of cyber adversaries and protect their critical assets from emerging threats.

Incident Detection and Response Strategies

Incident detection and response are core functions of a Security Operations Center (SOC), enabling organizations to identify and mitigate cyber threats before they cause significant damage. Cyberattacks continue to grow in complexity and frequency, making it critical for SOC teams to have well-defined strategies for detecting malicious activities and responding effectively. A strong incident detection and response framework minimizes downtime, protects sensitive data, and reduces the financial and reputational impact of security breaches.

Effective incident detection begins with comprehensive visibility across an organization's IT infrastructure. SOC teams rely on a combination of Security Information and Event Management (SIEM) systems, Intrusion Detection Systems (IDS), Intrusion Prevention Systems (IPS), Endpoint Detection and Response (EDR) solutions, and Network Detection and Response (NDR) tools to monitor security events in real time. These technologies continuously collect and analyze security logs, network traffic, and system activity to detect anomalies and indicators of compromise. Without full visibility, security incidents can go unnoticed, allowing attackers to move undetected within an organization's environment.

Threat intelligence plays a critical role in enhancing incident detection capabilities. SOC teams integrate external threat intelligence feeds with internal security monitoring tools to identify emerging threats, known attack signatures, and adversary tactics. By correlating security events with threat intelligence data, analysts can detect suspicious activities more accurately and prioritize incidents based on risk severity. Threat intelligence also helps security teams anticipate new attack trends, enabling them to proactively strengthen security controls before an attack occurs.

Behavioral analytics and machine learning improve incident detection by identifying deviations from normal system activity. Traditional security tools rely on rule-based detection, which can be effective for identifying known attack patterns but may struggle to detect zero-day threats and advanced persistent threats (APTs). Machine learning algorithms analyze historical data to establish baselines of normal behavior, allowing SOC teams to detect anomalies that may indicate a security breach. User and Entity Behavior Analytics (UEBA) enhances detection capabilities by identifying suspicious login attempts, privilege escalation, and data exfiltration attempts that deviate from typical user behavior.

Once a security incident is detected, SOC teams must respond swiftly to contain the threat and prevent further damage. Incident response follows a structured approach, typically based on established frameworks such as the National Institute of Standards and Technology (NIST) Incident Response Lifecycle or the SANS Incident Handling Process. These frameworks outline the essential phases of incident response, including preparation, detection, containment, eradication, recovery, and lessons learned. Each phase is critical to ensuring a coordinated and effective response to security incidents.

Containment is one of the most urgent steps in incident response, as it prevents the attacker from causing further harm. SOC teams must implement immediate countermeasures, such as isolating infected endpoints, blocking malicious IP addresses, and disabling compromised user accounts. Rapid containment limits the spread of malware, stops unauthorized access, and prevents data exfiltration. Containment strategies vary depending on the type and severity of the incident, and organizations must have predefined containment procedures to act quickly when an attack occurs.

Eradication involves removing the threat from the affected environment and eliminating the root cause of the incident. SOC teams conduct forensic investigations to determine how the attack occurred, what vulnerabilities were exploited, and whether any backdoors or persistence mechanisms were left behind by the attacker. This phase requires thorough log analysis, malware reverse engineering, and memory forensics to ensure that all traces of the threat are removed. If a vulnerability was exploited, security patches must be applied, and misconfigurations must be corrected to prevent future incidents.

Recovery focuses on restoring affected systems and services to normal operation. Organizations must ensure that all compromised systems are securely reinstated, whether through system restoration, backup recovery, or software reinstallation. Before returning systems to production, SOC teams must conduct validation testing to confirm that the threat has been fully eradicated. Security teams may also implement additional monitoring measures to detect any signs of reoccurrence. Recovery efforts should be carefully planned to minimize downtime and avoid disrupting business operations.

The lessons learned phase is crucial for strengthening an organization's overall security posture. After an incident is resolved, SOC teams conduct a post-incident analysis to evaluate the effectiveness of their response. This analysis helps identify gaps in security controls, areas where response times can be improved, and lessons that can be applied to future incidents. SOC teams document findings in an incident report, which includes details about the attack vector, impact assessment, response actions taken, and recommendations for improving security measures. Organizations should update incident response playbooks based on these findings to ensure continuous improvement.

Automation and orchestration significantly enhance the efficiency of incident detection and response. Security Orchestration, Automation, and Response (SOAR) platforms allow SOC teams to automate repetitive tasks such as alert triage, threat containment, and evidence collection. Automation reduces response times and alleviates the workload on analysts, enabling them to focus on high-priority incidents. SOAR platforms also integrate with SIEM systems and other security tools, streamlining the entire incident response workflow. By leveraging automation, organizations can improve response speed and consistency while reducing the likelihood of human error.

Collaboration and communication are essential for effective incident response. SOC teams must coordinate with IT teams, legal departments, compliance officers, and executive leadership to ensure a unified response to security incidents. Clear communication channels must be established to facilitate real-time information sharing and decision-making. In cases of large-scale incidents, organizations may need to involve external cybersecurity experts, law enforcement agencies, or regulatory bodies. Having a well-defined incident communication plan ensures that all stakeholders are informed and aligned in their response efforts.

Regular incident response exercises, such as tabletop simulations and red teaming assessments, help organizations test and refine their incident response strategies. These exercises simulate real-world attack scenarios, allowing SOC teams to practice their response procedures, identify weaknesses, and improve coordination. By conducting routine security drills, organizations enhance their readiness to handle actual cyber incidents and reduce response times. Continuous training and skill development for SOC analysts also play a vital role in ensuring that security teams remain prepared for evolving threats.

Incident detection and response strategies must continuously evolve to keep pace with the ever-changing threat landscape. Organizations must regularly assess their security tools, refine detection rules, and update response playbooks based on emerging threats. By combining advanced detection technologies, well-defined response procedures, automation, and ongoing training, SOC teams can effectively detect and mitigate cyber threats, reducing the overall risk to the organization. A proactive approach to incident detection and response strengthens cybersecurity resilience, minimizes the impact of security incidents, and ensures that organizations can quickly recover from cyberattacks while improving their long-term security posture.

Log Management and Data Retention Policies

Log management and data retention policies are fundamental aspects of cybersecurity operations within a Security Operations Center (SOC). Effective log management enables security teams to collect, store, analyze, and retrieve log data from various systems and applications, providing visibility into network activity, user behavior, and security events. Proper data retention policies ensure that logs are preserved for an appropriate duration, meeting regulatory requirements and supporting forensic investigations. Without a structured approach to log management and retention, organizations risk losing critical security insights, failing compliance audits, and reducing their ability to respond effectively to cyber threats.

A SOC relies on centralized log collection to aggregate security event data from multiple sources, including firewalls, intrusion detection systems (IDS), security information and event management (SIEM) platforms, endpoint detection and response (EDR) tools, authentication servers, cloud environments, and application logs. This centralized approach allows analysts to correlate security events across different systems, detect anomalies, and investigate potential threats. The volume of log data generated daily can be enormous, requiring SOCs to implement efficient log storage and indexing mechanisms to ensure quick retrieval and analysis when needed.

Log data serves as the primary source of evidence in security investigations. When a cyber incident occurs, security analysts examine logs to reconstruct the sequence of events, identify the initial point of compromise, and determine the extent of the attack. Network logs help track malicious traffic, endpoint logs reveal unauthorized access attempts, and system logs provide insights into potential misconfigurations or vulnerabilities exploited by attackers. By maintaining comprehensive log records, SOC teams can conduct forensic investigations that enable them to understand attack patterns, mitigate threats, and strengthen security controls.

The quality of log data is just as important as its volume. Collecting excessive or irrelevant logs can overwhelm security teams and make it difficult to identify meaningful security events. Organizations must define clear logging policies to ensure that only relevant data is collected. Logs should capture key details such as timestamps, source and destination IP addresses, user activity, authentication attempts, and changes to critical system configurations. Proper log categorization helps streamline analysis, allowing security analysts to focus on high-priority events rather than sifting through an excessive number of benign logs.

Data retention policies dictate how long logs should be stored and when they should be archived or deleted. These policies vary based on industry regulations, legal requirements, and business needs. Some regulations, such as the General Data Protection Regulation (GDPR) and the California Consumer Privacy Act (CCPA), impose strict data retention and deletion rules to protect user privacy. Other regulatory frameworks, including the Payment Card Industry Data Security Standard (PCI DSS), the Health Insurance Portability and Accountability Act (HIPAA), and the Sarbanes-Oxley Act (SOX), mandate that security logs be retained for specific periods to ensure compliance with audit and reporting requirements. Organizations must carefully assess applicable regulations and establish retention policies that balance security, compliance, and data storage costs.

Short-term log retention policies are typically used for active security monitoring and incident response. SOC teams require access to recent logs for real-time threat detection, alert correlation, and security investigations. These logs are stored in high-performance, searchable databases that allow analysts to quickly retrieve and analyze data as security events unfold. Short-term log retention periods may range from 30 days to six months, depending on operational requirements and security needs.

Long-term log retention is necessary for forensic investigations, regulatory audits, and historical threat analysis. While recent logs provide immediate security insights, historical logs help security teams identify trends, detect persistent threats, and analyze attack patterns over time. Some compliance frameworks require organizations to retain logs for several years, ensuring that forensic data is available in case of a delayed breach discovery or legal investigation. Long-term log storage solutions must balance accessibility with cost efficiency, often utilizing cloud storage, tape backups, or cold storage solutions to retain logs securely without excessive infrastructure costs.

Log integrity and protection are essential components of data retention policies. Cybercriminals often attempt to erase or manipulate log data to cover their tracks, making it critical for organizations to implement tamper-resistant logging mechanisms. Immutable storage solutions, cryptographic hashing, and secure access controls help ensure that log data remains unaltered and trustworthy. Encrypting logs during transit and at rest protects them from unauthorized access and data breaches. SOC teams should regularly audit log storage systems to verify that logs are being retained correctly and have not been modified.

The scalability of log management infrastructure is another key consideration for SOCs. As organizations expand their digital footprint, the volume of generated log data increases exponentially. Traditional on-premises log storage solutions may become insufficient over time, leading many organizations to adopt cloud-based log management platforms. Cloud-based solutions offer elasticity, allowing organizations to scale storage capacity based on demand while benefiting from built-in redundancy and high availability. Hybrid log storage models, which combine on-premises and cloud storage, provide flexibility and resilience by ensuring that critical logs remain accessible even in the event of infrastructure failures.

Automation plays a significant role in modern log management and data retention strategies. Security orchestration, automation, and response (SOAR) platforms enhance log management by automating log collection, correlation, and analysis. Automated log parsing and enrichment help SOC analysts extract meaningful insights from raw log data, reducing the time required for incident investigation. Machine learning algorithms can identify patterns and anomalies in log data, improving the detection of sophisticated threats that may evade traditional rule-based security measures. By leveraging automation, SOC teams can efficiently manage large volumes of logs while maintaining high accuracy in threat detection.

Regular log review and analysis are critical for identifying potential security risks and refining detection capabilities. SOC teams should conduct routine log audits to identify gaps in log collection, optimize logging configurations, and ensure compliance with retention policies. Threat hunting exercises often involve analyzing historical log data to uncover signs of previously undetected intrusions. By continuously monitoring and refining log management processes, organizations can improve their ability to detect and respond to cyber threats in a timely manner.

Well-defined log management and data retention policies enable SOCs to maintain visibility into security events, support forensic investigations, and meet compliance requirements. Organizations must implement scalable, secure, and efficient log storage solutions to ensure that critical security data is available when needed. By balancing short-term and long-term log retention, protecting log integrity, leveraging automation, and conducting regular audits, SOC teams can optimize their log management strategies and enhance their overall cybersecurity posture.

Network Security Monitoring Best Practices

Network security monitoring is a critical function within a Security Operations Center (SOC) that enables organizations to detect, analyze, and respond to cyber threats in real time. As cyberattacks continue to evolve in complexity, organizations must implement best practices to ensure their network security monitoring is effective and capable of identifying malicious activities before they escalate into full-scale breaches. A well-structured network security monitoring strategy enhances visibility, improves threat detection, and reduces the risk of data breaches and operational disruptions.

The foundation of network security monitoring is comprehensive visibility into all network traffic. Organizations must ensure that they have full coverage of their network infrastructure, including internal and external traffic, cloud environments, remote connections, and encrypted data flows. Without complete visibility, security teams risk overlooking potential threats that may be hiding within unmonitored segments of the network. Deploying network taps, span ports, and traffic mirroring solutions ensures that all relevant data is captured and analyzed in real time. Visibility must extend to all devices, including endpoints, servers, virtual machines, Internet of Things (IoT) devices, and third-party integrations, to provide a holistic view of network activity.

Intrusion Detection Systems (IDS) and Intrusion Prevention Systems (IPS) play a crucial role in network security monitoring by detecting and blocking malicious network activity. IDS solutions passively monitor network traffic and generate alerts when suspicious patterns are identified, while IPS solutions actively block threats in real time. These tools help security teams detect reconnaissance activities, unauthorized access attempts, and known attack signatures. Regularly updating IDS/IPS signatures and tuning detection rules is essential to ensuring these systems remain effective against emerging threats. Organizations should also deploy behavior-based anomaly detection alongside traditional signature-based methods to identify zero-day threats and advanced persistent threats (APTs).

Log correlation and Security Information and Event Management (SIEM) integration enhance the effectiveness of network security monitoring by aggregating data from multiple sources. SIEM systems collect logs from firewalls, routers, switches, authentication servers, and endpoint security tools to provide a centralized view of security events. Correlating network traffic data with system logs and user activity allows security teams to detect lateral movement, privilege escalation, and potential insider threats. SIEM platforms apply correlation rules and machine learning algorithms to identify anomalies and prioritize security incidents, reducing the number of false positives and improving incident response times.

Threat intelligence integration strengthens network security monitoring by providing real-time data on known attack vectors, malicious IP addresses, and indicators of compromise (IOCs). By leveraging external and internal threat intelligence feeds, SOC teams can enhance their detection capabilities and respond to threats more effectively. Threat intelligence platforms continuously update threat indicators, enabling organizations to proactively block malicious domains, detect phishing attempts, and identify command-and-control (C2) communications. Security teams should integrate threat intelligence into their network monitoring tools to automatically flag suspicious activities that match known attack patterns.

Encryption analysis is an essential aspect of network security monitoring, as cybercriminals increasingly use encrypted communication channels to evade detection. While encryption protects sensitive data, it also presents a challenge for security teams trying to inspect network traffic for malicious content. Organizations must implement decryption capabilities for inbound and outbound traffic while ensuring compliance with privacy regulations. Transport Layer Security (TLS) inspection, Secure Sockets Layer (SSL) decryption, and deep packet inspection (DPI) enable security teams to analyze encrypted network traffic without compromising legitimate data security. Configuring decryption policies correctly ensures that malicious activities hidden within encrypted traffic are detected while minimizing impact on network performance.

Network segmentation enhances security monitoring by limiting the movement of attackers within an organization's environment. By dividing the network into segments based on function, access level, or sensitivity, organizations can reduce the risk of unauthorized lateral movement and contain potential security incidents. Micro-segmentation further refines access control by implementing granular security policies that restrict communication between devices and applications. Security teams must monitor inter-segment traffic to detect unauthorized access attempts, privilege escalations, and data exfiltration activities. Implementing strict access controls and least-privilege principles further enhances network segmentation effectiveness.

Behavioral analytics and machine learning improve network security monitoring by identifying deviations from normal network activity. Traditional security tools often rely on static rules and predefined attack signatures, which may not be sufficient to detect emerging threats. Machine learning algorithms analyze historical traffic patterns, identify baselines of normal activity, and detect anomalies that may indicate a security threat. User and Entity Behavior Analytics (UEBA) solutions enhance network monitoring by identifying unusual login attempts, abnormal data transfers, and suspicious network access behaviors. These insights enable security teams to detect insider threats, compromised accounts, and sophisticated cyberattacks that evade traditional detection methods.

Automated response and Security Orchestration, Automation, and Response (SOAR) platforms streamline network security monitoring by enabling real-time incident containment. Automation reduces the manual workload on security analysts by executing predefined response actions when a security threat is detected. For example, if a SIEM system identifies an unauthorized data transfer, a SOAR platform can automatically isolate the affected endpoint, revoke user access, and notify the security team. Automated playbooks improve response speed, reduce human error, and enhance overall network security posture. Organizations should continuously refine their automated response workflows to adapt to evolving threats and operational requirements.

Continuous network traffic analysis is critical for detecting advanced threats and persistent attack campaigns. Security teams should implement real-time packet capture (PCAP) solutions to analyze raw network data and identify suspicious activities that may not generate traditional security alerts. Network flow analysis tools, such as NetFlow and sFlow, provide additional insights into traffic patterns, bandwidth usage, and abnormal communication behaviors. By continuously monitoring network traffic and correlating findings with historical data, organizations can detect slow-moving attacks, botnet activity, and data exfiltration attempts that may otherwise go unnoticed.

Incident response coordination is a key component of effective network security monitoring. Organizations must establish clear incident response procedures, escalation protocols, and communication workflows to ensure that security events are handled efficiently. Security teams should conduct regular network security drills and tabletop exercises to test their response readiness and refine their strategies. Collaborating with IT, compliance, and legal teams ensures that network security incidents are managed in accordance with regulatory requirements and business continuity objectives. Maintaining detailed network security monitoring logs also supports forensic investigations and helps organizations learn from past incidents.

Network security monitoring best practices must evolve alongside emerging threats and technological advancements. Organizations should continuously assess their monitoring capabilities, update detection rules, and refine security policies to stay ahead of cyber adversaries. A proactive approach to network security monitoring, combined with automation, threat intelligence, and behavioral analytics, strengthens an organization's ability to detect, analyze, and respond to cyber threats effectively. By implementing these best practices, SOC teams can improve network visibility, enhance threat detection, and reduce the risk of security breaches in an increasingly complex cybersecurity landscape.

Endpoint Detection and Response (EDR)

Endpoint Detection and Response (EDR) is a critical component of modern cybersecurity, enabling organizations to detect, investigate, and respond to threats at the endpoint level. As cyber threats become more sophisticated, attackers increasingly target endpoints such as laptops, desktops, servers, and mobile devices to gain initial access to networks, escalate privileges, and exfiltrate sensitive data. Traditional antivirus solutions and signature-based security tools are no longer sufficient to combat advanced threats. EDR solutions provide enhanced visibility, real-time monitoring, and automated response capabilities, making them essential for Security Operations Centers (SOCs) in defending against modern cyberattacks.

The primary function of EDR is to continuously monitor endpoint activities and detect suspicious behaviors that may indicate a security threat. Unlike traditional security solutions that rely on predefined signatures to detect known malware, EDR solutions use behavioral analysis, heuristics, and machine learning to identify anomalies that could indicate an ongoing attack. This proactive approach enables SOC teams to detect zero-day threats, fileless malware, and advanced persistent threats (APTs) that may evade conventional security measures. By analyzing system processes, network connections, file modifications, and registry changes, EDR solutions provide detailed insights into endpoint activities, allowing analysts to correlate security events and identify potential compromises.

Real-time threat detection is a key advantage of EDR technology. Cyberattacks can unfold rapidly, and the ability to detect malicious activities as they happen is crucial in preventing widespread damage. EDR solutions continuously collect and analyze telemetry data from endpoints, identifying indicators of compromise (IOCs) and indicators of attack (IOAs). When a suspicious activity is detected, the EDR system generates alerts and provides contextual information that helps SOC analysts investigate the threat. This real-time detection capability enables security teams to respond swiftly, reducing the time attackers have to operate within an environment.

Threat hunting is another important function of EDR, allowing security teams to proactively search for threats that may have bypassed automated detection mechanisms. SOC analysts use EDR platforms to conduct in-depth investigations, analyzing endpoint behaviors and searching for hidden indicators of compromise. Threat hunters can query historical endpoint data, examine attack patterns, and identify anomalies that could indicate stealthy adversary activities. By leveraging threat intelligence and behavioral analytics, SOC teams can uncover previously undetected threats, strengthening the organization's overall security posture.

Incident response and containment capabilities are essential features of EDR solutions. When a security incident occurs, SOC teams must act quickly to contain the threat and prevent further damage. EDR platforms enable security analysts to isolate compromised endpoints, terminate malicious processes, and remove suspicious files without disrupting business operations. Automated response actions, such as blocking network connections or rolling back unauthorized system changes, help mitigate threats before they escalate. The ability to remotely quarantine infected endpoints reduces the risk of lateral movement within the network, preventing attackers from compromising additional systems.

Forensic investigation and root cause analysis are enhanced by EDR technology, providing SOC teams with the data needed to understand how an attack occurred and what vulnerabilities were exploited. EDR solutions store detailed endpoint activity logs, allowing analysts to reconstruct attack timelines, trace adversary movements, and identify initial entry points. By analyzing forensic data, security teams can determine whether the attack was part of a larger campaign, assess the impact on the organization, and implement measures to prevent future incidents. The ability to conduct rapid and thorough forensic investigations is critical in minimizing the long-term consequences of security breaches.

Integration with other security tools enhances the effectiveness of EDR solutions. A well-integrated EDR system works in conjunction with Security Information and Event Management (SIEM) platforms, Security Orchestration, Automation, and Response (SOAR) solutions, and threat intelligence feeds to provide a holistic approach to cybersecurity. SIEM platforms aggregate logs from multiple sources, correlating endpoint data with network traffic and system events to provide a broader context for threat detection. SOAR platforms automate response workflows, ensuring that detected threats are handled consistently and efficiently. Threat intelligence integration allows EDR solutions to identify emerging attack patterns and apply proactive countermeasures.

Machine learning and artificial intelligence (AI) play a significant role in enhancing EDR capabilities. Traditional security tools often struggle to keep up with evolving threats, but AI-driven EDR solutions can analyze vast amounts of endpoint data to detect subtle anomalies that may indicate an attack. By continuously learning from historical attack data, AI-powered EDR systems improve their accuracy over time, reducing false positives and increasing detection efficiency. AI also enhances behavioral analytics, enabling EDR platforms to recognize deviations from normal endpoint activity and detect sophisticated attacks that rely on stealth and evasion techniques.

The shift toward cloud-based and remote work environments has increased the importance of EDR in securing distributed endpoints. Traditional perimeter-based security approaches are no longer sufficient as employees access corporate resources from various locations and devices. Cloud-native EDR solutions provide centralized visibility and control over endpoints, regardless of their physical location. These solutions enable SOC teams to monitor remote devices, enforce security policies, and respond to incidents without requiring physical access to the affected systems. As organizations embrace hybrid work models, cloud-based EDR becomes a critical component of endpoint security strategies.

Regulatory compliance and data protection requirements further highlight the necessity of EDR implementation. Many industries are subject to strict cybersecurity regulations that mandate continuous monitoring, incident reporting, and data protection measures. EDR solutions help organizations meet compliance requirements by providing detailed audit logs, automated threat detection, and incident response capabilities. Regulations such as the General Data Protection Regulation (GDPR), the Health Insurance Portability and Accountability Act (HIPAA), and the Payment Card Industry Data Security Standard (PCI DSS) require organizations to maintain strong endpoint security controls. EDR technology ensures that organizations can detect and respond to endpoint threats while maintaining compliance with industry standards.

Organizations must also address challenges related to EDR deployment and management. While EDR provides powerful security capabilities, it requires skilled personnel to configure, monitor, and respond to threats effectively. SOC teams must be trained to interpret EDR alerts, conduct investigations, and implement response actions efficiently. Additionally, EDR solutions generate large volumes of telemetry data, which can overwhelm security analysts if not properly filtered and prioritized. Implementing automation, fine-tuning detection rules, and leveraging threat intelligence can help organizations optimize their EDR deployment and maximize its effectiveness.

As cyber threats continue to evolve, Endpoint Detection and Response remains a crucial component of modern cybersecurity defense. By providing real-time visibility, advanced threat detection, automated response actions, and forensic investigation capabilities, EDR solutions enable SOC teams to detect and mitigate endpoint threats efficiently. Organizations that invest in robust EDR strategies enhance their ability to defend against cyberattacks, protect sensitive data, and maintain compliance with regulatory requirements. A well-implemented EDR solution strengthens an organization's overall security posture, ensuring that endpoints remain protected against the ever-growing landscape of cyber threats.

Cloud Security Monitoring in a SOC

Cloud security monitoring is a critical function within a Security Operations Center (SOC), ensuring that an organization's cloud environments remain protected from cyber threats. As businesses increasingly migrate workloads, applications, and data to the cloud, the security landscape has evolved, introducing new challenges and risks. Traditional security monitoring methods designed for on-premises infrastructure are no longer sufficient to detect and mitigate threats in cloud environments. SOC teams must adopt specialized cloud security monitoring strategies to maintain visibility, enforce security policies, and respond to incidents effectively in dynamic cloud architectures.

One of the key challenges of cloud security monitoring is the shared responsibility model, which defines security responsibilities between cloud service providers (CSPs) and customers. While CSPs are responsible for securing the underlying infrastructure, customers must protect their data, applications, and configurations. This means that organizations cannot rely solely on the cloud provider's security measures but must implement their own monitoring controls to detect misconfigurations, unauthorized access, and potential security breaches. SOC teams must have a clear understanding of their security responsibilities in Infrastructure-as-a-Service (IaaS), Platform-as-a-Service (PaaS), and Software-as-a-Service (SaaS) environments to establish effective monitoring strategies.

Visibility is a foundational aspect of cloud security monitoring. Unlike traditional networks, cloud environments are highly dynamic, with workloads scaling up and down based on demand. SOC teams must implement tools that provide real-time visibility into cloud resources, including virtual machines, containers, storage services, and identity access management configurations. Cloud-native security solutions such as Cloud Security Posture Management (CSPM), Cloud Workload Protection Platforms (CWPP), and Cloud Access Security Brokers (CASB) help monitor and enforce security policies across multi-cloud and hybrid environments. By integrating these tools into the SOC's monitoring framework, organizations can detect and remediate security issues before they escalate into incidents.

Identity and access management (IAM) monitoring is essential for securing cloud environments. Attackers often target IAM misconfigurations to gain unauthorized access to cloud resources. SOC teams must continuously monitor IAM policies, user activities, and privilege escalations to detect signs of account compromise or insider threats. Implementing multi-factor authentication (MFA), least privilege access controls, and logging all authentication events enhances cloud security. Additionally, SOC teams should monitor for anomalous login behaviors, such as access attempts from unfamiliar locations or multiple failed login attempts, which may indicate brute-force attacks or credential theft.

Cloud security monitoring relies on logging and event data collected from various cloud services. Cloud service providers offer built-in logging capabilities such as AWS CloudTrail, Microsoft Azure Monitor, and Google Cloud Audit Logs, which capture detailed records of security events, API calls, and system changes. These logs provide valuable insights into user activities, network traffic, and configuration modifications. SOC teams must centralize and analyze cloud logs using Security Information and Event Management (SIEM) platforms to detect suspicious patterns and correlate cloud events with other security data. Effective log management ensures that SOC teams can conduct forensic investigations, identify security incidents, and maintain compliance with regulatory requirements.

Threat detection in cloud environments requires specialized analytics and behavioral monitoring techniques. Traditional signature-based detection methods are less effective in cloud environments due to the dynamic nature of workloads and the use of ephemeral resources such as containers and serverless functions. SOC teams must leverage artificial intelligence (AI) and machine learning (ML) algorithms to analyze large volumes of cloud data and detect anomalies that may indicate potential threats. User and Entity Behavior Analytics (UEBA) enhances cloud security monitoring by identifying deviations from normal activity, such as unauthorized data transfers, unusual API calls, or privilege escalations. By detecting subtle indicators of compromise,

SOC teams can proactively respond to security incidents before attackers gain a foothold in the cloud environment.

Data security is a major concern in cloud environments, as organizations store sensitive information in cloud databases, object storage services, and file-sharing applications. SOC teams must implement data loss prevention (DLP) solutions to monitor data access, detect unauthorized transfers, and enforce encryption policies. Cloud security monitoring should include tracking data flows to prevent data exfiltration attempts by malicious insiders or external attackers. Enforcing encryption for data at rest and in transit, along with strict access controls, helps protect sensitive information from unauthorized exposure. Regular security audits and compliance assessments ensure that data security policies align with industry standards and regulatory requirements.

Container and serverless security monitoring has become increasingly important as organizations adopt modern cloud-native architectures. Containers, orchestrated by platforms like Kubernetes, introduce new security challenges such as insecure container images, misconfigurations, and vulnerabilities in containerized applications. SOC teams must monitor container activity, detect unauthorized modifications, and enforce security policies at the orchestration level. Serverless functions, while reducing the attack surface by eliminating traditional infrastructure management, still require monitoring to detect abnormal function executions, excessive API requests, and potential code injection attacks. Implementing cloud-native security tools designed for container and serverless monitoring helps organizations maintain a strong security posture in these environments.

Compliance and regulatory requirements influence cloud security monitoring strategies. Organizations operating in regulated industries must ensure that their cloud environments meet compliance standards such as the General Data Protection Regulation (GDPR), the Health Insurance Portability and Accountability Act (HIPAA), the Payment Card Industry Data Security Standard (PCI DSS), and the Federal Risk and Authorization Management Program (FedRAMP). Cloud security monitoring tools must provide audit trails, real-time compliance reporting, and automated enforcement of security policies to ensure adherence to regulatory requirements. SOC teams should regularly review cloud configurations, perform security assessments, and document security controls to demonstrate compliance.

Incident response in cloud environments requires rapid detection and containment strategies. Unlike on-premises infrastructure, where security teams have full control over network traffic and physical systems, cloud incident response depends on the ability to quickly identify threats, revoke access, and remediate misconfigurations. SOC teams must establish automated incident response workflows that can detect and isolate compromised cloud resources, terminate unauthorized sessions, and apply remediation actions in real time. Security Orchestration, Automation, and Response (SOAR) solutions enhance cloud incident response by enabling predefined playbooks to execute automated responses, reducing the time required to contain and mitigate threats.

Cloud security monitoring must also address supply chain risks, as organizations rely on third-party vendors, cloud applications, and external integrations that introduce potential security vulnerabilities. SOC teams should monitor cloud service dependencies, assess the security posture of third-party applications, and implement zero-trust security models to limit the impact of compromised external services. Continuous risk assessments, vendor security evaluations, and strict access control policies help reduce the risk of supply chain attacks in cloud environments.

Cloud environments are highly dynamic, requiring continuous security improvements and adaptive monitoring strategies. SOC teams must stay up to date with emerging cloud threats, evolving attack techniques, and advancements in cloud security technologies. Regular security training, red teaming exercises, and threat simulations help SOC analysts refine their skills and improve their ability to detect and respond to cloud-based threats. By integrating cloud security monitoring with automation, threat intelligence, and compliance frameworks, organizations can strengthen their cloud defenses, minimize security risks, and ensure the continuous protection of their cloud assets.

Building an Effective Threat Hunting Program

A well-structured threat hunting program is essential for proactively detecting and mitigating advanced cyber threats that may evade traditional security defenses. Unlike automated threat detection tools that rely on predefined signatures and behavioral analytics, threat hunting is a proactive, intelligence-driven approach that actively searches for hidden threats within an organization's network. Security Operations Centers (SOCs) implement threat hunting programs to identify advanced persistent threats (APTs), insider threats, and stealthy adversaries that operate below the radar of conventional security measures. Developing an effective threat hunting program requires a combination of skilled analysts, advanced tools, structured methodologies, and continuous improvement.

The foundation of a strong threat hunting program begins with defining clear objectives and goals. Organizations must determine the scope of their threat hunting efforts, identifying key assets, high-risk areas, and critical data that require enhanced protection. Threat hunters should focus on detecting previously undetected threats, reducing dwell time, and improving incident response readiness. A well-defined program aligns with the organization's overall cybersecurity strategy and integrates seamlessly with existing security operations, enhancing visibility and strengthening defense mechanisms against evolving cyber threats.

Threat intelligence plays a crucial role in guiding threat hunting activities. By leveraging threat intelligence feeds, security teams gain insights into the tactics, techniques, and procedures (TTPs) used by adversaries. Frameworks such as MITRE ATT&CK provide a structured approach to understanding attacker behaviors and mapping them to real-world attack scenarios. Threat hunters use intelligence-driven hypotheses to investigate potential attack vectors, identifying anomalies and indicators of compromise (IOCs) that may indicate an ongoing attack. By continuously updating threat intelligence sources, SOC teams ensure that their hunting techniques remain relevant and effective against emerging threats.

Data collection and analysis are critical components of threat hunting. SOC teams must aggregate data from multiple sources, including endpoint logs, network traffic, authentication records, and cloud activity. Security Information and Event Management (SIEM) platforms serve as central repositories for log data, allowing threat hunters to query, correlate, and analyze security events in real time. Endpoint Detection and Response (EDR) solutions provide detailed insights into process executions, file modifications, and registry changes, helping analysts detect suspicious activities on compromised endpoints. Network Detection and Response (NDR) tools enhance visibility into network traffic, detecting lateral movement, command-and-control (C2) communications, and data exfiltration attempts. A comprehensive data collection strategy ensures that threat hunters have access to relevant and actionable security information.

Threat hunting methodologies are structured approaches that guide analysts in uncovering hidden threats. The hypothesis-driven approach involves formulating a hypothesis based on threat intelligence and investigating specific attack techniques. For example, an analyst may hypothesize that an attacker is using stolen credentials to move laterally within the network and then test this hypothesis by analyzing authentication logs for unusual access patterns. Another approach is known as indicator-driven hunting, which involves searching for IOCs such as malicious IP addresses, domain names, and file hashes obtained from threat intelligence sources. The analytics-driven approach uses machine learning and behavioral analysis to detect anomalies that deviate from established baselines. By combining these methodologies, SOC teams improve their ability to detect sophisticated cyber threats.

Automation enhances the efficiency of threat hunting by accelerating data analysis and reducing manual workloads. Security Orchestration, Automation, and Response (SOAR) platforms integrate with SIEM, EDR, and NDR tools to automate the collection and correlation of security data. Machine learning algorithms identify patterns in large datasets, helping analysts detect anomalies and potential security threats faster. Automated playbooks streamline investigative processes by executing predefined queries, collecting forensic artifacts, and triggering response actions when suspicious activities are detected. While automation significantly improves hunting efficiency, human expertise remains critical for interpreting complex attack patterns and making informed decisions.

Threat hunting requires a high level of skill and expertise, making continuous training and knowledge sharing essential for success. Organizations must invest in training programs that equip analysts with advanced forensic investigation skills, malware analysis techniques, and adversary simulation knowledge. Red teaming exercises help threat hunters develop an attacker mindset, improving their ability to identify and counteract malicious activities. Participating in cybersecurity conferences, sharing hunting techniques with industry peers, and contributing to threat intelligence communities enhance the collective knowledge of SOC teams. Organizations should foster a culture of continuous learning, encouraging analysts to refine their skills and adapt to emerging threats.

Collaboration between different security teams strengthens the effectiveness of a threat hunting program. Threat hunters work closely with incident response teams to validate findings, contain threats, and implement mitigation strategies. Security engineers provide technical expertise to optimize log collection, refine detection rules, and enhance security infrastructure. Red teams simulate attack scenarios that challenge threat hunters to detect and respond to adversary tactics in real-world conditions. Effective communication between threat hunting, blue teaming, and red teaming efforts ensures a well-coordinated defense strategy.

Measuring the success of a threat hunting program requires defining key performance indicators (KPIs) that evaluate hunting effectiveness. Metrics such as dwell time reduction, number of incidents detected through proactive hunting, false positive rates, and time to resolution help organizations assess the impact of their threat hunting efforts. By continuously monitoring and refining these metrics, SOC teams can identify areas for improvement and enhance the overall efficiency of their hunting operations. Regular post-hunting reviews and documentation of findings contribute to the continuous evolution of threat detection capabilities.

A mature threat hunting program evolves over time, incorporating lessons learned from past incidents and adapting to new attack techniques. Organizations must regularly reassess their threat hunting strategies, update detection rules, and enhance their security monitoring infrastructure to stay ahead of adversaries. By leveraging automation, advanced analytics, and human expertise, SOC teams build a proactive security posture that minimizes risk and strengthens resilience against cyber threats. A well-executed threat hunting program not only improves threat detection capabilities but also enhances an organization's overall cybersecurity defense strategy.

Security Orchestration, Automation, and Response (SOAR)

Security Orchestration, Automation, and Response (SOAR) is a critical technology that enhances the efficiency of Security Operations Centers (SOCs) by automating repetitive security tasks, streamlining incident response workflows, and improving overall threat detection and mitigation. As cyber threats continue to grow in complexity, SOC teams face an increasing volume of alerts, requiring them to quickly identify, analyze, and respond to potential security incidents. Without automation, security analysts must manually investigate each alert, leading to fatigue, slow response times, and increased risk of missing critical threats. SOAR platforms enable organizations to optimize their security operations by integrating various security tools, automating workflows, and orchestrating incident response actions in a coordinated manner.

A fundamental component of SOAR is security orchestration, which involves integrating multiple security tools and technologies to work together seamlessly. Modern SOCs rely on various security solutions, including Security Information and Event Management (SIEM) systems, Endpoint Detection and Response (EDR) platforms, Intrusion Detection Systems (IDS), firewalls, threat intelligence feeds, and ticketing systems. Without orchestration, analysts must manually switch between these tools, leading to inefficiencies and increased response times. SOAR platforms unify security operations by connecting these tools through standardized workflows, enabling data sharing and coordinated actions across different security layers. This orchestration ensures that threat intelligence is shared in real time, allowing SOC teams to detect and mitigate threats more effectively.

Automation is another critical aspect of SOAR, reducing the manual effort required to handle security incidents. Many security tasks, such as log analysis, threat enrichment, alert triage, and initial incident response, are repetitive and time-consuming. SOAR platforms leverage automation to execute these tasks without human intervention, allowing security analysts to focus on more complex investigations and strategic security initiatives. For example, if a SIEM system generates an alert for a suspected phishing attack, a SOAR platform can automatically extract indicators of compromise (IOCs) from the email, check the sender's reputation against threat intelligence databases, and block the malicious domain on the organization's firewall. By automating these routine processes, SOC teams improve their efficiency and reduce response times.

Incident response is a core function of SOAR, enabling organizations to respond to security threats in a structured and consistent manner. Traditional incident response processes often involve multiple teams and require extensive coordination, leading to delays in containment and mitigation efforts. SOAR platforms provide predefined playbooks that standardize response procedures, ensuring that incidents are handled consistently and effectively. Playbooks define step-by-step actions for various security scenarios, such as ransomware attacks, data breaches, insider threats, and credential theft. When a security incident is detected, the SOAR platform automatically executes the appropriate playbook, coordinating actions across different security tools and teams to contain the threat as quickly as possible.

Threat intelligence integration enhances the effectiveness of SOAR by providing real-time data on known attack vectors, malicious actors, and evolving cyber threats. By connecting with threat intelligence feeds, SOAR platforms can automatically enrich security alerts with contextual information, helping analysts determine the severity of an incident and prioritize response actions. For example, if a suspicious IP address is detected attempting to access a critical system, the SOAR platform can query threat intelligence sources to determine whether the IP is associated with known cybercriminal activities. If confirmed as malicious, the platform can automatically update firewall rules, notify security teams, and trigger additional monitoring for related attack indicators.

Machine learning and artificial intelligence (AI) further enhance SOAR capabilities by improving threat detection, decision-making, and automated response actions. AI-driven SOAR platforms analyze historical security data to identify patterns, predict potential attack scenarios, and recommend optimized response strategies. Machine learning algorithms continuously refine automated workflows, reducing false positives and improving the accuracy of threat detection. By leveraging AI, SOC teams can prioritize high-risk threats, adapt to emerging attack techniques, and enhance their ability to detect sophisticated cyber threats that may evade traditional security controls.

SOAR platforms also improve collaboration and communication within SOC teams and across different departments within an organization. Security incidents often require coordination between IT teams, compliance officers, legal departments, and executive leadership. Without a structured communication framework, critical information may be delayed or lost, impacting the effectiveness of incident response efforts. SOAR solutions provide centralized dashboards, automated notifications, and integrated ticketing systems that facilitate real-time collaboration and decision-making. Security teams can assign tasks, track incident progress, and document response actions in a unified system, ensuring a coordinated and transparent security operation.

One of the key benefits of SOAR is its ability to reduce alert fatigue, a major challenge faced by SOC analysts. Security monitoring tools generate thousands of alerts daily, many of which are false positives or low-priority events. Manually reviewing and investigating each alert is not feasible, leading to delayed responses and missed critical threats. SOAR platforms automate alert triage by applying predefined rules, prioritizing high-risk alerts, and eliminating redundant notifications. By filtering out noise and focusing on actionable threats, SOAR helps analysts make faster and more informed decisions, improving the overall efficiency of security operations.

Compliance and regulatory requirements are additional factors that make SOAR an essential tool for modern SOCs. Organizations must adhere to industry regulations such as the General Data Protection Regulation (GDPR), the Health Insurance Portability and Accountability Act (HIPAA), the Payment Card Industry Data Security Standard (PCI DSS), and other cybersecurity standards. SOAR platforms assist with compliance by automating log collection, audit reporting, and policy enforcement. Security teams can generate compliance reports, track incident response metrics, and ensure that security operations align with regulatory requirements. By standardizing security workflows and maintaining detailed audit trails, SOAR simplifies compliance management and reduces the risk of regulatory penalties.

As cyber threats continue to evolve, organizations must continuously refine their security strategies to stay ahead of attackers. Implementing a SOAR platform enhances a SOC's ability to detect, investigate, and respond to threats in a timely and efficient manner. By integrating security orchestration, automation, and response into daily operations, SOC teams can reduce operational overhead, improve incident response times, and strengthen overall cybersecurity posture. Organizations that invest in SOAR technology gain a significant advantage in managing security threats, enabling them to proactively defend against cyberattacks and maintain resilience in an increasingly hostile threat landscape.

Managing and Mitigating False Positives

False positives are a significant challenge in the daily operations of a Security Operations Center (SOC), leading to wasted time, analyst fatigue, and reduced efficiency in responding to actual security threats. A false positive occurs when a security monitoring tool incorrectly classifies a benign event as a potential security incident. While robust security monitoring systems are designed to detect threats accurately, the increasing complexity of cyberattacks and network environments often results in high volumes of alerts, many of which turn out to be false positives. Managing and mitigating these false positives is essential for ensuring that security teams focus their efforts on genuine threats while maintaining an effective and efficient SOC.

One of the primary reasons for false positives is overly aggressive security configurations. Many security tools, including intrusion detection systems (IDS), endpoint detection and response (EDR) solutions, and Security Information and Event Management (SIEM) platforms, are configured with default or overly broad detection rules that may trigger alerts for normal system activities. For example, an IDS might flag encrypted traffic as suspicious, even if it is legitimate business communication. Similarly, a SIEM system may generate alerts for common administrative actions, such as a user accessing a sensitive system, when the activity is routine. Fine-tuning these security tools by adjusting detection rules, defining clear thresholds, and applying contextual analysis helps reduce unnecessary alerts while maintaining strong security defenses.

Contextual awareness is key to mitigating false positives. Security alerts should be analyzed within the broader context of network behavior, user activity, and system logs. Without context, a security event that appears suspicious in isolation may actually be a normal occurrence. For instance, if a user logs in from an unfamiliar location, it may initially trigger a security alert. However, if additional data shows that the user previously authenticated via a virtual private network (VPN) or regularly travels for work, the alert may be unnecessary. SOC teams can integrate User and Entity Behavior Analytics (UEBA) to establish behavioral baselines and reduce alerts triggered by normal activities.

Threat intelligence integration plays an important role in filtering out false positives. By comparing security events against real-world threat intelligence feeds, SOC teams can determine whether an alert corresponds to a known malicious indicator or if it is likely a benign anomaly. For example, if a firewall detects an attempted connection to an external IP address, but the IP is associated with a well-known and trusted service, the alert can be deprioritized. Conversely, if the IP is linked to a command-and-control (C2) server used in malware campaigns, the alert should be escalated for further investigation. Effective use of threat intelligence helps SOC teams distinguish between genuine threats and benign network activity.

Automation and Security Orchestration, Automation, and Response (SOAR) platforms can significantly reduce false positives by streamlining alert triage and incident response. Automation enables SOC teams to apply predefined rules that classify and prioritize alerts based on historical data, severity levels, and correlation with other security events. For example, if a SIEM platform generates an alert for unusual user activity, a SOAR system can automatically check whether the same user has exhibited similar behavior in the past and whether the event aligns with known attack patterns. If no indicators of compromise are found, the alert can be deprioritized, reducing the workload on analysts.

Regularly updating security detection rules and signatures is essential to maintaining an effective balance between detecting real threats and reducing false positives. Many security tools rely on predefined signatures to detect known attack patterns, but these signatures can become outdated or misaligned with an organization's specific network environment. SOC teams should conduct periodic reviews of detection rules, refine alert parameters, and eliminate redundant or overly sensitive rules that generate excessive false positives. Collaborating with security vendors to fine-tune threat detection algorithms ensures that security tools remain effective without overwhelming analysts with unnecessary alerts.

Improving the accuracy of security monitoring requires continuous feedback loops between SOC analysts and security engineers. Analysts who review alerts daily can provide valuable insights into recurring false positives, helping engineers adjust detection configurations and optimize monitoring systems. Implementing a structured feedback process allows SOC teams to document patterns in false positive alerts and refine detection mechanisms accordingly. Over time, this iterative approach improves the precision of security monitoring tools, ensuring that alerts are more relevant and actionable.

Machine learning and artificial intelligence (AI) are increasingly being leveraged to mitigate false positives by improving threat detection accuracy. AI-driven security analytics can identify patterns in historical security events, recognize normal behaviors, and flag only those deviations that truly indicate potential threats. Unlike traditional rule-based security monitoring, which generates alerts based on fixed parameters, AI can adapt to evolving attack techniques and distinguish between legitimate activity and actual security incidents. Implementing AI-driven security analytics within a SOC helps filter out low-priority alerts while enhancing the detection of real threats.

User training and security awareness programs also contribute to reducing false positives. Employees who understand cybersecurity best practices are less likely to trigger false alerts through common mistakes, such as using weak passwords, repeatedly failing login attempts, or accessing company resources through unsecured networks. Educating staff on proper security protocols, phishing awareness, and secure authentication methods helps prevent unnecessary security alerts related to user errors. Encouraging employees to report suspicious activities rather than relying solely on automated security monitoring can also help improve the accuracy of incident detection.

Continuous monitoring and periodic assessment of security tools ensure that false positive rates remain manageable. Organizations should establish key performance indicators (KPIs) to track false positive rates, alert resolution times, and the ratio of legitimate threats to non-threatening security events. By regularly analyzing these metrics, SOC teams can identify trends, adjust detection thresholds, and optimize security workflows to improve operational efficiency. Reducing false positives enhances the effectiveness of the SOC, allowing analysts to focus their efforts on investigating genuine security incidents rather than wasting time on false alarms.

Managing and mitigating false positives is an ongoing process that requires a combination of advanced security technologies, fine-tuned detection mechanisms, automation, and human expertise. By refining security configurations, integrating threat intelligence, leveraging AI, and continuously improving detection accuracy, SOC teams can reduce alert fatigue and enhance their ability to detect and respond to actual cyber threats. An optimized security monitoring approach ensures that organizations can maintain a strong defense against cyberattacks while minimizing unnecessary disruptions caused by excessive false positive alerts.

Digital Forensics and Investigations in a SOC

Digital forensics is a crucial function within a Security Operations Center (SOC), enabling organizations to investigate cyber incidents, uncover evidence, and determine the root cause of security breaches. When an organization experiences a cyberattack, digital forensics provides the structured methodology needed to analyze compromised systems, identify malicious activities, and reconstruct the sequence of events leading up to the incident. A well-executed forensic investigation not only helps resolve ongoing security incidents but also strengthens an organization's defenses against future attacks by identifying vulnerabilities and weaknesses in its security posture.

A SOC must have the capability to conduct forensic investigations in real time to respond to active threats while also performing post-incident analysis to assess the full impact of security breaches. Digital forensics in a SOC involves collecting and analyzing data from various sources, including endpoint devices, network traffic, system logs, cloud environments, and external threat intelligence feeds. The ability to quickly and accurately analyze forensic data is essential for mitigating risks, recovering compromised systems, and supporting legal or regulatory actions when necessary.

One of the key principles of digital forensics is the preservation of evidence. When an incident occurs, SOC teams must follow strict procedures to ensure that forensic data is not altered or contaminated during the investigation process. This requires creating forensic images of affected systems, capturing volatile memory data, and securing log files before any further analysis is conducted. Any unauthorized modification of forensic evidence can compromise the integrity of an investigation and may render the findings inadmissible in legal proceedings. For this reason, SOC analysts must use specialized forensic tools and techniques to ensure data integrity and chain of custody.

Forensic investigations often begin with the analysis of system logs and network traffic data. Security Information and Event Management (SIEM) platforms serve as a central repository for collecting and analyzing log data from firewalls, intrusion detection systems (IDS), authentication servers, and endpoint security tools. By correlating log entries, SOC analysts can identify patterns that indicate unauthorized access, privilege escalation, data exfiltration, or malware execution. Examining log timestamps and event sequences allows investigators to reconstruct attacker movements within an organization's network, revealing how the intrusion occurred and what actions were taken.

Memory forensics plays a critical role in analyzing advanced threats that may not leave traces in traditional logs or file systems. When a cyberattack involves fileless malware, rootkits, or in-memory exploits, forensic analysts must capture and analyze volatile memory (RAM) to uncover hidden malicious processes, encryption keys, and active network connections. Memory forensic tools allow SOC teams to extract evidence from running processes, analyze injected code, and detect unauthorized modifications to system memory. This technique is particularly useful in detecting sophisticated attacks that attempt to evade detection by avoiding disk-based artifacts.

Endpoint forensics focuses on analyzing individual devices, such as employee workstations, servers, and mobile devices, to uncover indicators of compromise (IOCs) and malicious activities. SOC analysts examine file system changes, registry modifications, scheduled tasks, and user activity logs to determine whether an endpoint has been compromised. In ransomware investigations, forensic analysis of endpoint systems helps identify the initial infection vector, determine whether sensitive data was encrypted or exfiltrated, and assess the effectiveness of containment measures. Endpoint Detection and Response (EDR) solutions enhance forensic capabilities by providing real-time monitoring, historical telemetry, and automated response actions.

Network forensics involves the capture and analysis of network traffic to detect suspicious communications, identify command-and-control (C2) channels, and trace the origin of attacks. Packet capture (PCAP) analysis allows SOC analysts to inspect raw network traffic, extract malicious payloads, and reconstruct attacker communications. Network Detection and Response (NDR) solutions enhance forensic investigations by applying behavioral analytics to network traffic, detecting anomalies, and identifying potential threats in encrypted communications. By analyzing network forensics data, SOC teams can uncover hidden attack techniques, track lateral movement, and prevent data exfiltration.

Cloud forensics is becoming increasingly important as organizations migrate workloads to cloud environments. Investigating security incidents in the cloud presents unique challenges due to the distributed nature of cloud services, shared responsibility models, and limited access to raw system data. SOC teams must leverage cloud-native forensic tools, such as AWS CloudTrail, Microsoft Azure Security Center, and Google Cloud Audit Logs, to collect evidence and analyze security events. Cloud forensics investigations focus on detecting unauthorized access to cloud resources, identifying misconfigurations that may have led to a breach, and analyzing API calls for suspicious activity. Effective cloud forensics requires close collaboration with cloud service providers and adherence to industry best practices for securing cloud environments.

Incident response and forensic investigations go hand in hand, as forensic analysis provides the intelligence needed to contain and remediate security incidents. When a SOC detects an active threat, forensic investigators work alongside incident response teams to determine the scope of the attack, assess the impact on business operations, and implement mitigation strategies. Forensic analysis helps answer critical questions such as how the attacker gained entry, what data was accessed or stolen, and whether backdoors or persistence mechanisms were left behind. The findings from forensic investigations inform future security improvements, helping organizations strengthen their defenses against similar attack techniques.

Legal and regulatory considerations are an important aspect of digital forensics in a SOC. Many industries are subject to compliance requirements that mandate proper handling, storage, and reporting of forensic evidence. Regulations such as the General Data Protection Regulation (GDPR), the Health Insurance Portability and Accountability Act (HIPAA), and the Payment Card Industry Data Security Standard (PCI DSS) require organizations to maintain audit trails, conduct forensic investigations after security incidents, and report breaches to regulatory authorities. Ensuring compliance with these regulations requires SOC teams to document forensic findings meticulously, maintain proper chain of custody, and follow established legal procedures for handling digital evidence.

The effectiveness of digital forensics in a SOC depends on continuous skill development, training, and the use of advanced forensic tools. SOC analysts must stay updated on emerging attack techniques, forensic methodologies, and legal considerations through ongoing training programs, hands-on exercises, and participation in cybersecurity communities. Red teaming and tabletop exercises help SOC teams refine their forensic investigation capabilities by simulating real-world attack scenarios. Additionally, investing in forensic toolsets, such as disk imaging software, memory analysis tools, and network forensic platforms, enhances the SOC's ability to conduct thorough and accurate investigations.

By integrating digital forensics into SOC operations, organizations improve their ability to detect, investigate, and mitigate security incidents. A well-defined forensic investigation process enables SOC teams to uncover hidden threats, trace attacker activities, and enhance security defenses based on real-world attack data. Digital forensics not only helps resolve security incidents but also contributes to a proactive cybersecurity strategy that minimizes risks, strengthens organizational resilience, and ensures compliance with regulatory requirements.

Red Team vs. Blue Team Operations

In cybersecurity, the constant evolution of threats requires organizations to adopt proactive defense strategies to test and strengthen their security posture. One of the most effective ways to achieve this is through Red Team vs. Blue Team operations, a structured approach where offensive and defensive security teams simulate real-world cyberattacks and responses. This dynamic exercise helps organizations identify vulnerabilities, improve incident response capabilities, and enhance overall security resilience. Red and Blue Teams operate with different objectives but work towards a common goal: strengthening the organization's defenses against real cyber threats.

The Red Team operates as the offensive security force, simulating the actions of real-world attackers. This team consists of ethical hackers, penetration testers, and security researchers who attempt to exploit weaknesses in an organization's infrastructure, applications, and security controls. The primary goal of the Red Team is to think like adversaries, using tactics, techniques, and procedures (TTPs) commonly employed by cybercriminals, advanced persistent threats (APTs), and nation-state actors. By conducting realistic attack simulations, the Red Team helps uncover security gaps that may not be evident through standard vulnerability assessments or automated security tools.

Red Team operations typically begin with reconnaissance, where team members gather intelligence about the target organization. This phase involves open-source intelligence (OSINT) gathering, social engineering, network scanning, and identifying publicly exposed assets. Once reconnaissance is complete, the team attempts to exploit weaknesses using various attack vectors, such as phishing emails, credential stuffing, lateral movement techniques, and privilege escalation. The Red Team's goal is to infiltrate the network, bypass security controls, and achieve predefined objectives, such as accessing sensitive data, compromising user accounts, or demonstrating persistence within the environment.

The Blue Team, on the other hand, is responsible for defending the organization's systems, networks, and data against cyber threats. Composed of SOC analysts, incident responders, security engineers, and threat hunters, the Blue Team continuously monitors security alerts, analyzes network traffic, and investigates suspicious activities. Their objective is to detect and mitigate attacks before they can cause significant damage. Blue Teams rely on security tools such as Security Information and Event Management (SIEM) platforms, Endpoint Detection and Response (EDR) solutions, Intrusion Detection Systems (IDS), and behavioral analytics to identify and respond to threats.

During Red Team vs. Blue Team exercises, the Blue Team must defend against simulated attacks without prior knowledge of the Red Team's tactics. This creates a realistic scenario where the defensive team must rely on its monitoring capabilities, threat intelligence, and incident response procedures to detect and contain adversary actions. The effectiveness of the Blue Team is measured by how quickly they identify threats, respond to security incidents, and prevent the Red Team from achieving its objectives. This type of exercise helps security teams improve their detection capabilities, refine their response strategies, and enhance their ability to counter real-world attacks.

One of the key challenges faced by the Blue Team is distinguishing between normal activity and malicious behavior. Cyberattacks often blend in with legitimate network traffic, making it difficult to identify threats without generating excessive false positives. The Blue Team must leverage advanced threat detection techniques, including behavioral analytics, anomaly detection, and correlation of security events, to accurately identify malicious activities. By analyzing attacker movements, Blue Team members can adjust their security monitoring tools, refine detection rules, and improve their ability to recognize sophisticated attack patterns.

Collaboration and continuous improvement are essential in Red Team vs. Blue Team operations. After an exercise, both teams conduct a post-engagement review, commonly known as a Purple Teaming session. This phase allows Red and Blue Teams to share insights, discuss the effectiveness of attack and defense techniques, and identify areas for improvement. The Red Team provides feedback on which security controls were successfully bypassed, while the Blue Team shares lessons learned from detecting and mitigating attacks. This iterative process enhances the organization's overall cybersecurity resilience by addressing weaknesses and implementing more effective defensive strategies.

Threat intelligence plays a significant role in enhancing both Red and Blue Team operations. The Red Team uses intelligence on emerging attack trends to develop realistic attack scenarios, ensuring that their tactics mirror those of real adversaries. The Blue Team, in turn, relies on threat intelligence to stay ahead of evolving threats, identify indicators of compromise (IOCs), and proactively strengthen defenses. Integrating real-time threat intelligence into security operations enables both teams to operate in a continuously evolving threat landscape, improving their ability to anticipate and respond to cyber threats effectively.

Automation and Security Orchestration, Automation, and Response (SOAR) platforms further enhance Red and Blue Team exercises by streamlining attack simulations and incident response workflows. The Red Team can use automated attack frameworks, such as MITRE ATT&CK adversary emulation tools, to replicate known attack techniques and assess the effectiveness of security controls. The Blue Team can leverage automation to speed up alert triage, correlation of security events, and containment actions. By integrating automation into these exercises, organizations can improve response efficiency and optimize security operations.

The benefits of Red Team vs. Blue Team operations extend beyond cybersecurity professionals. These exercises help executive leadership understand the organization's security risks and preparedness levels. By demonstrating the potential impact of cyberattacks and measuring the effectiveness of security defenses, organizations can justify investments in cybersecurity tools, personnel training, and security policy enhancements. Additionally, regulatory compliance frameworks, such as GDPR, HIPAA, and PCI DSS, require organizations to conduct regular security assessments and improve incident response capabilities, making Red and Blue Team operations a valuable component of compliance initiatives.

As cyber threats become more sophisticated, organizations must move beyond traditional security measures and adopt proactive security testing methodologies. Red Team vs. Blue Team exercises provide an effective way to identify weaknesses, enhance detection and response capabilities, and ensure that security teams are prepared for real-world attacks. By fostering collaboration between offensive and defensive security teams, organizations create a continuous improvement cycle that strengthens their cybersecurity posture, reduces the risk of breaches, and ensures resilience against emerging threats.

Implementing Threat Modeling in a SOC

Threat modeling is a proactive cybersecurity approach that enables Security Operations Centers (SOCs) to identify, analyze, and mitigate potential threats before they materialize into security incidents. By systematically evaluating the attack surface, threat actors, and vulnerabilities, SOC teams can develop targeted defense strategies to protect critical assets. Implementing threat modeling within a SOC enhances its ability to anticipate risks, prioritize security efforts, and strengthen overall resilience against cyber threats. A well-structured threat modeling process aligns with an organization's security objectives, providing a strategic framework for improving threat detection, incident response, and risk mitigation.

One of the fundamental principles of threat modeling is understanding the organization's attack surface. The attack surface consists of all entry points that could be exploited by an adversary, including networks, endpoints, applications, cloud services, and user access controls. SOC teams must continuously assess the attack surface to identify potential weaknesses that could be leveraged by attackers. This involves mapping out the organization's digital infrastructure, cataloging assets, and determining which components are most susceptible to compromise. By gaining visibility into the attack surface, SOC analysts can better anticipate potential attack vectors and allocate security resources more effectively.

Identifying threat actors is a critical step in the threat modeling process. Different organizations face different types of adversaries, ranging from financially motivated cybercriminals and insider threats to nation-state actors and hacktivist groups. SOC teams must analyze threat intelligence data to understand the motives, capabilities, and techniques of potential attackers. Frameworks such as MITRE ATT&CK provide valuable insights into common tactics, techniques, and procedures (TTPs) used by adversaries. By mapping known attack methods to the organization's infrastructure, SOC teams can determine which threats pose the greatest risk and develop countermeasures to defend against them.

Once the attack surface and potential threat actors are identified, the next step in threat modeling is assessing vulnerabilities within the organization's security environment. Vulnerabilities can exist in various forms, including unpatched software, misconfigured security controls, weak authentication mechanisms, and insufficient monitoring capabilities. SOC teams should conduct vulnerability assessments and penetration testing to identify security gaps that could be exploited. Understanding these vulnerabilities allows SOC analysts to simulate attack scenarios, test detection mechanisms, and implement proactive security controls to mitigate risks.

Threat modeling frameworks provide structured methodologies for assessing and mitigating threats. Several widely used frameworks help SOC teams analyze security risks systematically. The STRIDE model, developed by Microsoft, categorizes threats into six primary types: Spoofing, Tampering, Repudiation, Information Disclosure, Denial of Service, and Elevation of Privilege. This model helps SOC teams evaluate security weaknesses in applications, networks, and systems by identifying how different threat types could impact the organization. The DREAD model, another commonly used framework, assesses risks based on five factors: Damage potential, Reproducibility, Exploitability, Affected users, and Discoverability. By assigning risk scores to potential threats, SOC teams can prioritize remediation efforts based on impact and likelihood.

Integrating threat modeling into SOC workflows enhances the effectiveness of security monitoring and incident response. SOC teams can use threat models to develop threat detection rules, configure Security Information and Event Management (SIEM) systems, and refine alert triage processes. For example, if threat modeling reveals that a specific type of privilege escalation attack is likely, SOC teams can implement advanced monitoring rules to detect unusual privilege changes and enforce stricter access controls. By aligning threat detection capabilities with modeled threats, SOC teams can reduce false positives while improving detection accuracy.

Threat modeling also plays a key role in enhancing incident response preparedness. By simulating realistic attack scenarios, SOC teams can refine response playbooks, test containment strategies, and ensure that security controls function as intended. Security Orchestration, Automation, and Response (SOAR) platforms can leverage threat modeling insights to automate response workflows, enabling faster and more efficient threat mitigation. For example, if a threat model predicts that attackers may attempt to exfiltrate sensitive data using a compromised account, automated response actions can be configured to detect and block unauthorized data transfers in real time.

Collaboration between different security teams is essential for successful threat modeling implementation. Threat intelligence analysts provide insights into emerging threats, penetration testers validate security controls through adversary simulation, and SOC analysts integrate threat models into real-time monitoring and response operations. Additionally, security architects and engineers play a crucial role in designing secure systems based on threat modeling findings. By fostering collaboration across these teams, organizations can create a unified security strategy that incorporates proactive threat mitigation measures.

Threat modeling should be an ongoing process rather than a one-time exercise. As cyber threats evolve, organizations must continuously refine their threat models to adapt to new attack techniques and security challenges. Regular threat intelligence updates, vulnerability assessments, and red teaming exercises ensure that SOC teams stay ahead of adversaries. By embedding threat modeling into the SOC's daily operations, organizations can improve their ability to anticipate and mitigate threats before they lead to security incidents.

Regulatory compliance and risk management also benefit from threat modeling. Many cybersecurity regulations and industry standards require organizations to conduct risk assessments and implement proactive security measures. Compliance frameworks such as the General Data Protection Regulation (GDPR), the National Institute of Standards and Technology (NIST) Cybersecurity Framework, and the Payment Card Industry Data Security Standard (PCI DSS) emphasize the importance of identifying and mitigating security risks. Threat modeling provides organizations with a structured approach to assessing compliance risks, implementing security controls, and demonstrating due diligence in protecting sensitive data.

Automation and artificial intelligence (AI) further enhance threat modeling by analyzing vast amounts of security data, identifying patterns, and predicting potential attack paths. Machine learning algorithms can process threat intelligence feeds, correlate security events, and generate predictive threat models that help SOC teams prioritize risks. AI-driven threat modeling tools provide real-time recommendations on security configurations, helping organizations proactively address vulnerabilities before they can be exploited. By leveraging AI and automation, SOC teams can scale their threat modeling efforts, improve accuracy, and reduce manual workload.

An effective threat modeling program provides SOC teams with a proactive approach to cybersecurity, enabling them to anticipate, detect, and respond to threats with greater precision. By systematically analyzing attack surfaces, identifying threat actors, assessing vulnerabilities, and implementing structured threat models, organizations can strengthen their security posture. Continuous refinement of threat models, integration with security monitoring and incident response processes, and collaboration across security teams ensure that SOCs remain resilient against evolving cyber threats. A well-implemented threat modeling framework empowers organizations to shift from reactive security measures to proactive threat defense, reducing risk and enhancing overall cybersecurity readiness.

Developing SOC Playbooks and Standard Operating Procedures

Security Operations Centers (SOCs) must operate with consistency, efficiency, and accuracy to effectively detect, investigate, and respond to security incidents. One of the most critical components of a well-functioning SOC is the development of comprehensive playbooks and Standard Operating Procedures (SOPs). These structured documents provide clear guidelines on handling security incidents, reducing response times, minimizing errors, and ensuring that all security personnel follow a standardized approach to incident management. Playbooks and SOPs enhance an organization's ability to address cybersecurity threats in a systematic and repeatable manner, improving overall security posture and operational efficiency.

SOC playbooks are predefined, step-by-step guides that outline specific actions to be taken in response to various security incidents. They serve as tactical workflows that security analysts follow to identify, contain, mitigate, and remediate threats. Playbooks help SOC teams respond quickly and consistently to security events, ensuring that no critical steps are missed during an investigation. By standardizing response actions, playbooks reduce the reliance on individual expertise and provide a clear framework for handling incidents across all experience levels within the SOC.

Playbooks are typically categorized based on different types of security incidents. Common playbooks include those for phishing attacks, malware infections, insider threats, distributed denial-of-service (DDoS) attacks, unauthorized access attempts, and data breaches. Each playbook includes clearly defined procedures, starting from initial detection through containment, eradication, and recovery. By structuring incident response workflows in this manner, SOC teams can quickly assess the severity of an event, take appropriate actions, and escalate incidents when necessary.

The creation of effective SOC playbooks requires input from multiple stakeholders, including SOC analysts, incident responders, security engineers, and compliance officers. The first step in developing a playbook is identifying common threat scenarios that the organization is likely to face. SOC teams analyze historical incidents, threat intelligence reports, and risk assessments to determine the most relevant security threats. Each playbook must align with the organization's specific security infrastructure, tools, and operational requirements. By customizing playbooks to reflect the organization's environment, SOC teams can ensure that response actions are practical and actionable.

Standard Operating Procedures (SOPs) complement SOC playbooks by defining the overarching guidelines for security operations. While playbooks focus on specific incidents, SOPs establish general processes that govern daily security monitoring, log analysis, incident classification, threat intelligence integration, and communication protocols. SOPs provide consistency across all SOC functions, ensuring that security personnel follow best practices when handling security-related tasks. Clear and well-documented SOPs help new analysts onboard quickly and provide a reference for experienced staff to maintain compliance with organizational policies.

SOPs outline critical responsibilities within the SOC, including incident classification and severity levels. By categorizing security incidents based on predefined criteria, SOC teams can prioritize response efforts effectively. For example, an attempted brute-force attack on a non-critical system may be classified as a low-priority event, whereas an active ransomware infection targeting production servers would be treated as a high-severity incident requiring immediate escalation. Having clearly defined severity levels ensures that SOC teams allocate resources efficiently and respond appropriately to each type of incident.

One of the key benefits of playbooks and SOPs is their role in automating security operations. Security Orchestration, Automation, and Response (SOAR) platforms integrate with SOC playbooks to automate routine security tasks, reducing manual effort and improving response speed. Automated playbooks allow security tools to execute predefined actions, such as blocking malicious IP addresses, quarantining infected endpoints, and generating alerts for security teams. By leveraging automation, SOC teams can focus on high-priority incidents while minimizing the burden of repetitive tasks.

The effectiveness of SOC playbooks and SOPs depends on continuous improvement and regular updates. Cyber threats evolve rapidly, and outdated procedures can lead to inefficient or ineffective responses. SOC teams must review and refine playbooks based on lessons learned from real incidents, changes in attack techniques, and advancements in security technologies. Conducting regular tabletop exercises and incident simulations helps validate the effectiveness of playbooks and identifies areas for enhancement. Feedback from security analysts, penetration testers, and red team exercises ensures that SOC procedures remain relevant and aligned with emerging threats.

SOC playbooks and SOPs also play a crucial role in regulatory compliance and audit readiness. Many industries are subject to cybersecurity regulations that require organizations to implement standardized security procedures and incident response plans. Compliance frameworks such as the General Data Protection Regulation (GDPR), the National Institute of Standards and Technology (NIST) Cybersecurity Framework, the Health Insurance Portability and Accountability Act (HIPAA), and the Payment Card Industry Data Security Standard (PCI DSS) mandate proper incident documentation and response protocols. Well-documented playbooks and SOPs help organizations demonstrate compliance with these regulations, reducing legal and financial risks associated with security incidents.

Communication protocols are an essential component of SOC playbooks and SOPs. During security incidents, clear and efficient communication ensures that response teams coordinate effectively, stakeholders are informed, and escalation procedures are followed. Playbooks define communication workflows, including who should be notified, when notifications should be sent, and what information must be included in incident reports. Establishing predefined communication channels prevents confusion during high-pressure situations and ensures that security incidents are managed with transparency and accountability.

Playbooks also facilitate knowledge sharing within the SOC, reducing reliance on individual expertise and enabling all security team members to follow best practices. In a fast-paced security environment, new analysts must be able to contribute effectively from day one. Playbooks provide structured guidance, helping junior analysts understand response procedures while allowing senior analysts to focus on complex investigations. By fostering a culture of continuous learning, SOC teams improve their overall capabilities and strengthen their resilience against cyber threats.

The integration of playbooks with threat intelligence platforms further enhances incident response effectiveness. By incorporating real-time threat intelligence feeds, SOC teams can enrich security alerts with contextual information, enabling faster decision-making. Playbooks that include threat intelligence integration can dynamically adjust response actions based on the severity and credibility of detected threats. This approach improves accuracy in threat detection and helps SOC teams prioritize incidents that pose the greatest risk to the organization.

A well-structured set of SOC playbooks and SOPs is essential for maintaining a high level of security readiness. By developing clear, actionable, and regularly updated procedures, organizations can ensure that their SOC operates efficiently, responds to threats effectively, and continuously adapts to the evolving cyber landscape.

Through automation, collaboration, and integration with security tools, playbooks and SOPs help SOC teams reduce response times, enhance decision-making, and improve overall cybersecurity resilience.

Compliance and Regulatory Requirements for SOCs

Security Operations Centers (SOCs) play a crucial role in protecting organizations from cyber threats, but their effectiveness is also closely tied to compliance with regulatory and industry standards. Compliance and regulatory requirements ensure that SOCs operate within legal frameworks, follow best security practices, and maintain accountability when handling sensitive information. Many industries have strict guidelines that mandate specific security measures, data protection policies, and incident response procedures. Organizations that fail to comply with these requirements may face financial penalties, reputational damage, and legal consequences. To build a fully functional and legally compliant SOC, security teams must understand the regulatory landscape, implement required controls, and continuously monitor their adherence to relevant laws and standards.

One of the most widely recognized cybersecurity frameworks is the General Data Protection Regulation (GDPR), which applies to organizations that process the personal data of European Union (EU) residents. GDPR mandates that SOCs implement strict data protection measures, ensure secure handling of personal information, and respond to data breaches within defined timelines. SOCs must monitor access to sensitive data, detect unauthorized access attempts, and establish mechanisms for reporting security incidents. Organizations subject to GDPR must also ensure that log management and data retention policies align with regulatory requirements, ensuring that security events involving personal data are properly recorded and stored securely.

The Health Insurance Portability and Accountability Act (HIPAA) sets stringent security and privacy standards for organizations handling protected health information (PHI) in the healthcare industry. SOCs operating in healthcare environments must implement safeguards to prevent unauthorized access to medical records, monitor systems for potential breaches, and ensure that incident response procedures are aligned with HIPAA's security rule. Security teams must encrypt PHI, apply strict access controls, and regularly audit systems to detect potential security violations. HIPAA also requires that organizations have formalized incident response plans and breach notification procedures in place to address security threats affecting patient data.

The Payment Card Industry Data Security Standard (PCI DSS) is a regulatory framework that applies to organizations that process, store, or transmit credit card information. SOCs responsible for protecting payment data must comply with PCI DSS requirements by implementing access controls, monitoring for fraudulent activities, and encrypting cardholder information. Security teams must also conduct vulnerability assessments, apply security patches regularly, and restrict network access to authorized personnel. One of the key aspects of PCI DSS compliance is continuous security monitoring, which requires SOCs to detect unauthorized transactions, respond to potential fraud, and report security incidents affecting payment systems.

The National Institute of Standards and Technology (NIST) Cybersecurity Framework provides a set of best practices for managing cybersecurity risks across industries. Many government agencies and private sector organizations use NIST guidelines to structure their security programs and improve incident response capabilities. SOCs leveraging the NIST framework must align their operations with its core functions: Identify, Protect, Detect, Respond, and Recover. These guidelines help SOC teams develop proactive security measures, improve network monitoring, and enhance their ability to respond to cyber threats effectively. NIST also provides specific controls under the Special Publication 800-53 standard, which defines security requirements for federal information systems.

The Sarbanes-Oxley Act (SOX) focuses on financial reporting and requires organizations to maintain strong internal controls over financial systems. SOCs supporting SOX compliance must implement strict access controls, audit logging, and fraud detection mechanisms. Financial institutions and publicly traded companies are required to monitor activities that could affect the integrity of financial data and detect insider threats that may compromise accounting records. SOC analysts must ensure that security logs related to financial transactions are collected, stored securely, and reviewed regularly to detect anomalies that could indicate fraudulent activities.

The Federal Risk and Authorization Management Program (FedRAMP) is a compliance framework for cloud service providers working with U.S. government agencies. SOCs managing cloud security for government-related environments must follow FedRAMP requirements by ensuring data encryption, continuous security monitoring, and adherence to strict access control policies. Organizations must implement multi-factor authentication (MFA), secure cloud configurations, and real-time log analysis to detect unauthorized access attempts. FedRAMP also requires security assessments and regular audits to confirm that cloud environments meet federal security standards.

Another important regulation that affects SOC operations is the California Consumer Privacy Act (CCPA), which grants California residents rights over their personal data. SOCs managing security for organizations operating in California must ensure compliance by implementing data access controls, preventing unauthorized data sharing, and detecting security incidents that may expose consumer information. CCPA requires businesses to report data breaches, allowing affected individuals to take legal action if their personal data is mishandled. SOC teams must maintain detailed logs of security events, track access to sensitive information, and ensure that automated detection mechanisms are in place to identify potential data privacy violations.

Many SOCs also follow guidelines established by the International Organization for Standardization (ISO), particularly ISO/IEC 27001, which defines best practices for information security management systems (ISMS). SOCs implementing ISO 27001 must establish risk management processes, define security controls, and continuously monitor compliance with the standard. This framework emphasizes a structured approach to identifying security threats, mitigating risks, and documenting security policies. SOCs following ISO 27001 guidelines benefit from improved security governance, structured security policies, and enhanced risk management practices.

To maintain compliance with regulatory requirements, SOCs must implement structured auditing and reporting mechanisms. Security teams should regularly conduct compliance audits, assess security controls, and verify that log management practices align with regulatory mandates. Automated compliance monitoring tools help SOCs track adherence to security policies, generate compliance reports, and provide real-time visibility into regulatory gaps. Organizations should also establish compliance training programs to ensure that SOC analysts and security personnel understand their responsibilities and follow established security protocols.

Incident response plans play a vital role in meeting compliance requirements. Most regulations require organizations to have well-documented security incident response procedures, ensuring that SOC teams can quickly detect, analyze, and report security breaches. Compliance mandates often specify timeframes for reporting incidents to regulatory authorities, requiring SOC teams to maintain accurate records of detected threats and response actions. Having predefined incident response playbooks aligned with regulatory requirements improves coordination, reduces response times, and ensures compliance with legal obligations.

Regulatory requirements for SOCs continue to evolve as cyber threats become more sophisticated. Organizations must stay informed about changes in compliance laws, adapt their security policies, and invest in technologies that improve regulatory adherence. SOCs must integrate compliance into their daily security operations, ensuring that security monitoring, threat detection, and incident response processes align with industry standards. By maintaining compliance with legal and regulatory frameworks, organizations reduce security risks, protect sensitive data, and build a resilient cybersecurity infrastructure capable of withstanding evolving threats.

Security Metrics and Key Performance Indicators (KPIs)

Measuring the effectiveness of a Security Operations Center (SOC) is essential for ensuring that security teams operate efficiently, detect threats accurately, and respond to incidents in a timely manner. Security metrics and Key Performance Indicators (KPIs) provide SOC teams with quantifiable data to assess their performance, identify areas for improvement, and demonstrate the value of cybersecurity efforts to organizational leadership. Without clearly defined metrics, SOC operations risk becoming reactive and inefficient, making it difficult to measure progress or justify investments in security tools and personnel. By implementing a structured approach to security measurement, organizations can improve their security posture and optimize their threat detection and response capabilities.

Security metrics provide objective data on the performance of SOC operations, offering insight into security event trends, threat landscapes, and the effectiveness of security controls. These metrics help SOC teams make data-driven decisions, fine-tune security strategies, and ensure continuous improvement. KPIs, on the other hand, are specific measurements used to track the success of SOC initiatives against predefined goals. While security metrics provide raw data, KPIs focus on the outcomes that matter most to the organization. Defining meaningful KPIs ensures that SOC teams align their security efforts with business objectives and risk management priorities.

One of the most critical KPIs for a SOC is Mean Time to Detect (MTTD), which measures how long it takes for security analysts to identify a threat after it has entered the environment. A low MTTD indicates that the SOC is effectively monitoring security events and detecting threats quickly, minimizing the potential damage caused by cyberattacks. Conversely, a high MTTD suggests gaps in threat detection capabilities, which could allow attackers to remain undetected for extended periods. Improving MTTD requires continuous monitoring, refined detection rules, and the integration of threat intelligence to enhance visibility into emerging threats.

Mean Time to Respond (MTTR) is another key KPI that tracks the speed at which SOC teams contain and remediate security incidents after they are detected. A fast MTTR indicates that the SOC is efficiently handling incidents, reducing the dwell time of attackers within the network. Slow response times may indicate inefficiencies in incident handling processes, inadequate automation, or a lack of well-defined response playbooks. Enhancing MTTR involves streamlining incident response workflows, leveraging Security Orchestration, Automation, and Response (SOAR) platforms, and ensuring that security analysts have the tools and training needed to act quickly.

Mean Time to Contain (MTTC) measures how long it takes for SOC teams to isolate a threat and prevent further damage after an attack is detected. Containment is a crucial step in minimizing the impact of security incidents, as delays can result in attackers spreading laterally across the network, exfiltrating sensitive data, or deploying ransomware. Effective containment strategies involve automated threat isolation, network segmentation, and predefined incident response procedures that enable SOC teams to act decisively. Reducing MTTC helps limit the overall damage caused by cyber threats and strengthens an organization's ability to recover from security breaches.

False Positive Rate (FPR) is an important metric that indicates how often security alerts turn out to be non-threatening events. A high FPR suggests that security tools are generating excessive noise, leading to analyst fatigue and wasted resources. SOC teams must strike a balance between capturing legitimate threats and minimizing unnecessary alerts. Fine-tuning detection rules, leveraging machine learning for behavioral analysis, and integrating threat intelligence feeds can help reduce false positives and improve the accuracy of security monitoring. SOCs should also track the False Negative Rate (FNR), which measures how many real threats go undetected. A high FNR indicates that security defenses are failing to identify significant threats, leaving the organization vulnerable to cyberattacks.

Security Incident Volume is a metric that tracks the number of security alerts generated over a specific period. While a high volume of alerts may indicate a strong detection capability, it can also suggest that security tools are overly sensitive or that the organization is facing a surge in cyber threats. Analyzing incident volume helps SOC teams understand trends in attack frequency, detect patterns in malicious activity, and allocate resources effectively. Correlating incident volume with threat intelligence data provides additional context, enabling SOCs to distinguish between common security events and targeted attacks.

Dwell Time is another crucial metric that measures the duration an attacker remains undetected within a network. This metric is particularly important for identifying persistent threats and evaluating the effectiveness of security monitoring efforts. The longer an attacker remains undetected, the greater the risk of data exfiltration, system compromise, or business disruption. Reducing dwell time requires continuous threat hunting, enhanced anomaly detection, and real-time security analytics. SOC teams should focus on reducing dwell time by improving detection and response workflows, integrating automation, and enhancing endpoint visibility.

SOC analyst efficiency is a key KPI that evaluates how effectively security personnel handle security incidents. This metric can be measured by tracking the number of alerts reviewed, the number of incidents resolved, and the percentage of incidents escalated for further investigation. Analyst efficiency is influenced by the quality of security training, the usability of security tools, and the level of automation within the SOC. Investing in analyst training, optimizing workflows, and leveraging SOAR platforms can improve efficiency and reduce analyst burnout.

Threat Intelligence Utilization measures how effectively a SOC incorporates threat intelligence into its security operations. This KPI tracks the number of incidents detected based on threat intelligence feeds, the percentage of false positives reduced through intelligence enrichment, and the overall impact of intelligence-driven decision-making. SOC teams should continuously refine their threat intelligence strategies by integrating multiple sources, validating intelligence accuracy, and ensuring that intelligence is actionable and relevant to the organization's threat landscape.

Compliance Adherence is a critical metric for organizations that must comply with regulatory requirements and industry standards. This KPI evaluates how well the SOC meets compliance mandates such as

GDPR, HIPAA, PCI DSS, and NIST guidelines. Compliance adherence is measured through security audits, policy enforcement, and documentation of security events. Maintaining high compliance adherence demonstrates the organization's commitment to security best practices, reduces regulatory risks, and enhances overall cybersecurity resilience.

Measuring security metrics and KPIs ensures that SOCs operate with efficiency, accountability, and continuous improvement. By tracking these performance indicators, organizations can optimize their threat detection capabilities, reduce response times, and enhance their ability to mitigate security incidents. Security teams should regularly review and refine their KPIs, leveraging automation, machine learning, and threat intelligence to improve accuracy and effectiveness. A data-driven approach to SOC operations strengthens cybersecurity defenses, enables proactive threat management, and supports long-term security strategy planning.

The Role of Artificial Intelligence in a SOC

Artificial Intelligence (AI) is transforming the way Security Operations Centers (SOCs) detect, analyze, and respond to cyber threats. As cyberattacks become more sophisticated and frequent, SOC teams face increasing challenges in managing vast amounts of security data, identifying real threats among false positives, and responding to incidents in real time. Traditional security tools, which rely on predefined signatures and manual threat analysis, struggle to keep pace with evolving attack techniques. AI-powered solutions enhance SOC capabilities by automating threat detection, improving incident response efficiency, and providing deeper insights into emerging cyber risks.

One of the most significant applications of AI in a SOC is its ability to analyze massive volumes of security data at unprecedented speeds. Security monitoring tools generate thousands of alerts daily, many of which require human analysis to determine their severity. AI-driven systems use machine learning algorithms to process and correlate security events from multiple sources, including logs, network traffic, and endpoint activity. By applying pattern recognition and anomaly detection techniques, AI can identify suspicious behavior that may indicate an ongoing attack. This allows SOC analysts to focus on high-priority threats rather than spending time sifting through an overwhelming number of alerts.

AI enhances threat detection by identifying subtle attack patterns that traditional security tools may overlook. Machine learning models analyze historical attack data to recognize behaviors associated with known threats, while also detecting deviations from normal system activity. Unlike rule-based detection systems that rely on predefined signatures, AI continuously learns and adapts to new attack techniques. This is particularly useful for detecting zero-day threats, which exploit previously unknown vulnerabilities. AI-powered threat intelligence platforms aggregate data from global cybersecurity sources, enabling SOC teams to stay ahead of emerging threats and respond proactively.

User and Entity Behavior Analytics (UEBA) is a key area where AI significantly improves SOC operations. UEBA solutions leverage AI to establish baselines of normal behavior for users, devices, and applications within an organization. By continuously monitoring activity and comparing it against established baselines, AI can detect anomalies that may indicate insider threats, compromised credentials, or unauthorized access attempts. For example, if an employee's account suddenly logs in from an unfamiliar location or downloads an unusually large volume of data, AI-powered UEBA systems can flag the activity for further investigation. This approach minimizes false positives by considering context and behavioral patterns rather than relying solely on static security rules.

AI also plays a crucial role in automating incident response through Security Orchestration, Automation, and Response (SOAR) platforms. These systems integrate AI-driven decision-making with automated workflows to streamline threat containment and remediation. When a security incident is detected, AI can determine the severity of the threat and recommend response actions based on historical data. In some cases, AI-driven SOAR platforms can take autonomous actions, such as isolating compromised endpoints, blocking malicious IP addresses, or disabling affected user accounts. By reducing the need for manual intervention, AI helps SOC teams respond to threats faster and more efficiently, minimizing the impact of cyber incidents.

Predictive analytics is another area where AI enhances SOC effectiveness. Traditional security measures are often reactive, responding to threats after they have been detected. AI-powered predictive analytics leverages historical security data, attack patterns, and threat intelligence to anticipate potential threats before they occur. By identifying early warning signs of cyberattacks, SOC teams can implement preemptive security measures, such as strengthening access controls, patching vulnerabilities, or adjusting firewall rules. Predictive threat intelligence enables organizations to adopt a proactive cybersecurity strategy rather than merely reacting to security incidents as they unfold.

AI-driven malware analysis improves SOC capabilities by identifying and classifying malicious software more accurately. Traditional antivirus solutions rely on signature-based detection, which can be ineffective against polymorphic malware that constantly changes its code to evade detection. AI-powered malware detection systems use machine learning to analyze file behavior, identify suspicious code structures, and detect malware variants that do not match known signatures. AI also enhances sandboxing technologies by enabling dynamic behavioral analysis, where suspicious files are executed in a controlled environment to observe their actions before they can cause harm. This approach allows SOC teams to detect and neutralize sophisticated malware threats more effectively.

AI improves phishing detection by analyzing email communication patterns and identifying anomalies associated with phishing attacks. Phishing emails often bypass traditional email security filters by using social engineering tactics rather than malware attachments. AI-powered email security solutions analyze language patterns, sender reputation, and email metadata to detect phishing attempts. Natural Language Processing (NLP) algorithms assess the tone, structure, and intent of messages to identify fraudulent emails that attempt to deceive recipients into revealing sensitive information. AI-based phishing detection reduces the likelihood of users falling victim to phishing scams and enhances an organization's overall email security posture.

AI-powered deception technologies add an additional layer of security by deploying decoy assets, such as fake credentials, servers, or network shares, to mislead attackers. These deception techniques use AI to analyze attacker behavior and trigger alerts when unauthorized users interact with decoy systems. By luring adversaries into interacting with fake environments, SOC teams can gain valuable intelligence on attack methods, identify compromised accounts, and track adversary movements. AI-driven deception strategies enhance SOC threat detection by providing real-time visibility into active cyber threats while reducing the risk of actual asset compromise.

Despite its many advantages, AI implementation in SOC operations comes with challenges. Machine learning models require high-quality training data to improve their accuracy, and poorly trained models may generate false positives or overlook sophisticated attacks. Adversarial AI techniques, where cybercriminals manipulate AI models to evade detection, present an emerging threat that SOC teams must consider. Additionally, AI adoption requires skilled personnel who understand both cybersecurity and data science, highlighting the need for continuous training and expertise development within SOC teams.

AI-driven SOCs must also balance automation with human decision-making. While AI enhances efficiency and reduces response times, human analysts play a crucial role in interpreting complex security incidents, making judgment calls, and adapting security strategies based on evolving threats. Organizations must ensure that AI complements, rather than replaces, human expertise by providing analysts with enhanced visibility, decision-support tools, and actionable threat intelligence. SOC teams should establish feedback loops to refine AI models based on real-world threat data and continuously evaluate AI performance to prevent potential biases or inaccuracies.

As AI technology continues to advance, its role in SOC operations will become even more critical in combating modern cyber threats. Organizations that integrate AI into their security workflows benefit from improved threat detection accuracy, faster incident response, and greater operational efficiency. By leveraging AI-powered analytics, automation, and predictive intelligence, SOC teams can stay ahead of attackers and strengthen their cybersecurity defenses. AI is reshaping the future of SOC operations, enabling security teams to manage increasing cyber risks with greater precision, scalability, and resilience.

Managing Insider Threats in a SOC

Insider threats pose a significant risk to organizations, often more dangerous than external cyber threats because they originate from individuals with legitimate access to internal systems and data. Unlike external attackers who must bypass security defenses, insiders already have a level of trust within the organization, making their malicious actions harder to detect. A Security Operations Center (SOC) plays a crucial role in identifying, monitoring, and mitigating insider threats to protect sensitive information and maintain organizational security. Managing insider threats requires a combination of behavioral monitoring, access control policies, security awareness training, and automated threat detection techniques.

Insider threats can come in many forms, including employees, contractors, third-party vendors, or even former employees who still have access to company resources. Some insider threats are intentional, involving individuals who deliberately leak information, steal intellectual property, or sabotage systems for financial gain, personal revenge, or espionage. Others are unintentional, where employees accidentally expose sensitive data through misconfigurations, weak passwords, or phishing scams. Understanding the different types of insider threats allows SOC teams to develop tailored detection and response strategies to mitigate risks effectively.

One of the most effective ways to manage insider threats is through User and Entity Behavior Analytics (UEBA). UEBA solutions use machine learning and artificial intelligence to establish baselines of normal user behavior and detect deviations that may indicate malicious activity. If an employee suddenly downloads an unusually large volume of data, attempts to access unauthorized files, or logs in from a suspicious location, UEBA systems can trigger alerts for further investigation. By continuously monitoring user activities, SOC teams can identify insider threats early and take proactive measures before damage occurs.

Access control policies play a critical role in minimizing the risk of insider threats. Organizations should implement the principle of least privilege, ensuring that employees only have access to the resources necessary for their job functions. Privileged accounts, such as administrators and executives, should have additional security controls, including multi-factor authentication (MFA) and session monitoring. Role-based access control (RBAC) and attribute-based access control (ABAC) help enforce security policies by limiting user permissions based on job roles, responsibilities, and risk levels. Regular access reviews and audits ensure that permissions remain appropriate and that former employees no longer have access to company resources.

Data Loss Prevention (DLP) technologies help detect and prevent the unauthorized transmission of sensitive information. DLP solutions monitor network traffic, email communications, and endpoint activities for signs of data exfiltration, such as employees sending confidential files to personal email accounts or copying data to external USB devices. SOC teams can configure DLP policies to block, quarantine, or alert security analysts when suspicious data transfers occur. By implementing strict DLP controls, organizations reduce the risk of data leaks caused by malicious insiders or negligent employees.

Insider threats often exploit weak security awareness among employees. Many unintentional insider threats stem from human error, such as falling for phishing attacks, mishandling confidential information, or failing to follow security protocols. Regular security awareness training helps educate employees about cybersecurity risks, safe data handling practices, and how to recognize social engineering attacks. Employees should be encouraged to report suspicious activities, and organizations should foster a culture of security accountability where everyone understands their role in protecting sensitive information.

SOC teams must also monitor for privilege escalation and unauthorized access attempts. Insiders with malicious intent often try to elevate their privileges to gain access to restricted data or administrative controls. Security Information and Event Management (SIEM) platforms collect and analyze logs from authentication servers, endpoint security tools, and network devices to detect unauthorized privilege changes. Automated alerting systems notify SOC analysts when unusual access patterns occur, such as a user repeatedly attempting to access restricted systems or modifying account permissions without proper authorization.

Anomalous network activity is another indicator of potential insider threats. SOC teams should implement network traffic analysis and anomaly detection systems to identify suspicious behavior, such as employees accessing systems outside of normal working hours, transferring large amounts of data to unknown destinations, or connecting to external networks that are not part of the organization's infrastructure. Combining network detection and response (NDR) tools with endpoint detection and response (EDR) solutions enhances visibility into both network and endpoint activities, providing a comprehensive approach to insider threat monitoring.

The use of deception techniques can further enhance insider threat detection. Deploying honeypots, fake credentials, or decoy file servers can help SOC teams track insider movements and determine whether employees are attempting unauthorized access. If an insider interacts with decoy resources, SOC teams receive alerts and can investigate further to determine intent. These deception techniques provide valuable intelligence on potential threats while minimizing the risk to actual company assets.

Incident response planning is essential for managing insider threats effectively. Organizations must have predefined playbooks that outline how SOC teams should investigate, contain, and mitigate insider threats. These playbooks should include guidelines on handling insider investigations discreetly, as accusations of internal misconduct can have legal and reputational consequences. Collaboration with human resources, legal teams, and executive leadership ensures that insider threat incidents are addressed appropriately while maintaining compliance with company policies and employment laws.

Forensic investigations play a crucial role in handling insider threats. When a security breach is suspected, digital forensics teams must collect and analyze logs, endpoint data, and user activity records to reconstruct the events leading up to the incident. Forensic analysis helps determine whether an insider intentionally caused harm, if data was exfiltrated, and whether legal action should be taken. Maintaining an accurate chain of custody and preserving digital evidence ensures that forensic findings can be used in legal proceedings if necessary.

Regular audits and red team exercises help organizations assess their resilience to insider threats. Red teaming simulates real-world attack scenarios where ethical hackers attempt to exploit insider threat vulnerabilities. These exercises provide valuable insights into security weaknesses, test the effectiveness of detection mechanisms, and allow SOC teams to refine their incident response strategies. Conducting periodic security audits also ensures that insider threat detection policies and controls remain effective and aligned with evolving risks.

Organizations must also balance insider threat management with employee privacy and trust. Excessive surveillance or overly restrictive security measures can create a hostile work environment and reduce employee morale. Insider threat detection programs should be transparent, clearly communicated, and focused on protecting organizational assets rather than unnecessarily monitoring employee behavior. Implementing insider threat programs with ethical considerations and respecting employee privacy rights helps maintain trust while ensuring security objectives are met.

Managing insider threats in a SOC requires a multi-layered approach that combines behavioral analytics, access controls, data protection technologies, security awareness training, and proactive monitoring. By leveraging advanced detection techniques, implementing strict security policies, and fostering a security-conscious culture, organizations can minimize the risks associated with insider threats. Continuous evaluation and adaptation of insider threat management strategies ensure that SOC teams remain prepared to detect and mitigate internal security risks effectively.

Building a Security Awareness and Training Program

A well-structured security awareness and training program is an essential component of an organization's cybersecurity strategy. Human error remains one of the leading causes of security breaches, making it crucial to educate employees, contractors, and stakeholders about cybersecurity risks and best practices. A Security Operations Center (SOC) is responsible for monitoring threats, but without proper security awareness among employees, even the most advanced security technologies can fail. Building an effective security awareness and training program helps minimize risks, strengthen the organization's security posture, and create a culture of security-conscious behavior.

The foundation of a security awareness program begins with understanding the organization's specific risks and threats. Different industries face different cybersecurity challenges, so the training program must be tailored to address relevant risks. Organizations handling sensitive customer data must emphasize data protection and compliance requirements, while companies with extensive remote workforces need to focus on secure remote access and phishing awareness. Conducting a cybersecurity risk assessment allows security teams to identify the most critical threats and design training content that directly addresses these risks.

One of the key goals of a security awareness program is to educate employees on recognizing and responding to cyber threats. Phishing attacks, for example, are among the most common methods cybercriminals use to gain unauthorized access to systems. Employees must be trained to identify suspicious emails, avoid clicking on malicious links, and report potential phishing attempts to the SOC. Real-world phishing simulations help reinforce this training by exposing employees to simulated attacks and measuring their responses. Organizations that conduct regular phishing awareness exercises see a significant reduction in successful phishing attempts over time.

Password security is another critical aspect of security awareness training. Weak passwords and password reuse create vulnerabilities that attackers can exploit through brute-force attacks or credential-stuffing techniques. Employees should be trained on creating strong, unique passwords for different accounts and using password managers to securely store their credentials. Multi-factor authentication (MFA) should also be emphasized as an additional security measure to protect against unauthorized access, even if passwords are compromised. Organizations that enforce strong password policies and educate users on secure authentication practices significantly reduce the risk of credential-related breaches.

Security training should also cover the importance of secure data handling and confidentiality. Employees working with sensitive information must understand the risks associated with data exposure, accidental sharing, and improper storage. Guidelines on encrypting sensitive files, securing removable media, and restricting data access should be incorporated into training sessions. Employees should be aware of the consequences of data breaches, including legal implications, regulatory fines, and reputational damage to the organization. Reinforcing the importance of data protection helps create a security-conscious workforce that prioritizes safeguarding information assets.

A successful security awareness program must be engaging and interactive to ensure employees retain the information. Traditional training methods, such as lengthy PowerPoint presentations or generic online courses, often fail to capture employees' attention. Instead, organizations should implement interactive workshops, real-world scenarios, and hands-on exercises that encourage active participation. Gamification techniques, such as quizzes, challenges, and rewards, can make training sessions more engaging and increase information retention. Employees who find training interesting and relevant are more likely to apply security best practices in their daily work.

Regular training reinforcement is essential to maintaining a high level of security awareness. A one-time security training session is not sufficient to keep employees informed about evolving cyber threats. Organizations should implement ongoing training initiatives, such as monthly security newsletters, cybersecurity awareness posters, and short video tutorials that highlight recent security incidents and emerging threats. SOC teams should also conduct periodic security drills, such as simulated social engineering attacks or tabletop exercises, to reinforce training concepts and measure employee preparedness. Continuous education ensures that employees stay vigilant and up to date on the latest cybersecurity risks.

Security awareness training should also extend beyond employees to include third-party vendors, contractors, and business partners who have access to the organization's systems or data. Many security breaches occur due to weak security practices among third parties, making it essential to ensure that external collaborators follow the same security standards as internal employees. Organizations should establish security training requirements for vendors and contractors, conduct security audits, and enforce contractual agreements that outline security expectations. A holistic approach to security awareness ensures that all individuals interacting with company systems adhere to security best practices.

Executive leadership plays a crucial role in driving a strong security culture. If executives and senior management do not prioritize cybersecurity, employees are less likely to take security awareness training seriously. Leadership should actively participate in security training sessions, communicate the importance of cybersecurity to employees, and allocate resources to support ongoing security awareness initiatives. When executives demonstrate a commitment to security, it reinforces the message that cybersecurity is a shared responsibility across the entire organization.

Measuring the effectiveness of a security awareness and training program is essential for continuous improvement. SOC teams should track key performance indicators (KPIs) such as phishing simulation success rates, the number of security incidents caused by human error, and employee engagement levels in training sessions. Employee feedback surveys can also provide insights into the effectiveness of training materials and highlight areas that need improvement. Organizations should use this data to refine training content, address gaps, and continuously improve security awareness initiatives.

Compliance with regulatory and industry standards often requires organizations to implement security awareness training programs. Regulations such as the General Data Protection Regulation (GDPR), the Health Insurance Portability and Accountability Act (HIPAA), and the Payment Card Industry Data Security Standard (PCI DSS) mandate employee training on data protection and cybersecurity best practices. Failure to comply with these regulations can result in legal penalties and financial losses. SOC teams should ensure that security awareness programs align with regulatory requirements and maintain proper documentation of training activities to demonstrate compliance during audits.

Security awareness training should also emphasize the importance of reporting security incidents. Employees are often the first line of defense against cyber threats, and they must feel comfortable reporting suspicious activities without fear of punishment. Establishing clear reporting channels, such as a dedicated security hotline or email address, encourages employees to report security concerns promptly. SOC teams should respond to reported incidents efficiently, provide feedback to employees, and recognize individuals who contribute to improving security. A strong reporting culture enhances the organization's ability to detect and respond to threats quickly.

Building an effective security awareness and training program requires a strategic approach that combines education, engagement, reinforcement, and measurement. Organizations that invest in security awareness initiatives create a security-conscious workforce that actively participates in protecting company assets. By integrating security awareness into the organization's culture, regularly updating training content, and ensuring executive buy-in, SOC teams can significantly reduce cybersecurity risks and strengthen the organization's overall security posture.

Continuous Monitoring and Threat Adaptation

Continuous monitoring and threat adaptation are essential components of a modern Security Operations Center (SOC). Cyber threats evolve rapidly, and organizations must constantly assess and adjust their security posture to stay ahead of attackers. Traditional security approaches that rely on periodic assessments or static rules are no longer sufficient in an environment where new vulnerabilities, attack techniques, and malware variants emerge daily. A proactive security strategy requires real-time visibility, automated threat detection, and adaptive response mechanisms that allow SOC teams to respond to threats as they arise.

Continuous monitoring involves the ongoing collection, analysis, and correlation of security data from various sources across an organization's IT infrastructure. This includes logs from endpoints, network devices, cloud services, applications, and identity management systems. By continuously monitoring these environments, SOC teams gain a comprehensive view of security events, allowing them to detect suspicious activity in real time. Unlike traditional security assessments, which provide only a snapshot of an organization's security posture at a given moment, continuous monitoring ensures that potential threats are identified and addressed before they can cause significant harm.

One of the primary benefits of continuous monitoring is its ability to reduce dwell time, the period during which an attacker remains undetected in a network. Many cyberattacks involve an initial compromise followed by lateral movement, privilege escalation, and data exfiltration. Without continuous monitoring, attackers can operate undetected for weeks or even months, increasing the potential damage to the organization. By continuously analyzing network traffic, user behavior, and system logs, SOC teams can identify indicators of compromise (IOCs) early and take action before an attack progresses.

Threat adaptation is the process of evolving security measures based on emerging threats and intelligence. Cyber adversaries frequently modify their tactics, techniques, and procedures (TTPs) to bypass traditional security defenses. To counteract this, SOC teams must continuously update detection rules, refine security policies, and integrate real-time threat intelligence into their security operations. Threat intelligence feeds provide valuable insights into new malware strains, command-and-control (C2) servers, phishing campaigns, and attack methodologies. By integrating these insights into security monitoring tools, SOC teams can proactively block threats before they impact the organization.

Machine learning and artificial intelligence (AI) play a crucial role in continuous monitoring and threat adaptation. Traditional rule-based security systems can struggle to keep up with evolving threats, as they rely on predefined signatures and static detection methods. AI-driven security solutions analyze vast amounts of security data, identify anomalies, and detect patterns that may indicate malicious activity. Behavioral analytics enhance continuous monitoring by establishing baselines of normal user and system behavior, allowing SOC teams to detect deviations that could signal insider threats, compromised accounts, or advanced persistent threats (APTs).

Security automation further strengthens continuous monitoring efforts by reducing the manual workload on SOC analysts. Security Orchestration, Automation, and Response (SOAR) platforms integrate with continuous monitoring systems to automate incident triage, threat enrichment, and response actions. When an anomaly is detected, automation can trigger predefined response workflows, such as isolating a compromised endpoint, revoking user credentials, or blocking suspicious IP addresses. Automating these tasks enables SOC teams to respond to threats faster while minimizing human error and reducing the time attackers have to operate within the network.

Endpoint Detection and Response (EDR) solutions enhance continuous monitoring by providing deep visibility into endpoint activities. Attackers often target endpoints as entry points into an organization's infrastructure, making endpoint security a critical component of a SOC's monitoring strategy. EDR solutions continuously collect telemetry data from endpoints, identifying suspicious processes, unauthorized file modifications, and attempts to exploit vulnerabilities. By correlating endpoint data with network traffic analysis and threat intelligence, SOC teams can detect and mitigate sophisticated attacks that may bypass traditional perimeter defenses.

Cloud security monitoring is also an essential aspect of continuous monitoring, as organizations increasingly migrate workloads to cloud environments. Traditional security approaches designed for on-premises networks are not sufficient to protect dynamic cloud infrastructure, where resources scale up and down based on demand. Cloud-native security tools, such as Cloud Security Posture

Management (CSPM) and Cloud Workload Protection Platforms (CWPP), continuously monitor cloud configurations, API activity, and access controls for misconfigurations and security risks. By integrating cloud security monitoring with on-premises security operations, SOC teams can maintain visibility across hybrid environments and detect threats targeting cloud workloads.

Threat adaptation requires continuous refinement of security policies and incident response procedures. SOC teams must regularly review detection rules, update firewall policies, and adjust security controls based on emerging threats and evolving attack patterns. Conducting regular security assessments, such as red teaming and penetration testing, helps identify gaps in existing defenses and ensures that security measures remain effective. Lessons learned from past incidents should be documented and used to enhance SOC playbooks, enabling security teams to respond more efficiently to similar threats in the future.

Collaboration between SOC teams and other business units is essential for effective continuous monitoring and threat adaptation. Security teams must work closely with IT administrators, compliance officers, and executive leadership to ensure that security policies align with business objectives and regulatory requirements. Sharing threat intelligence with industry peers, government agencies, and cybersecurity organizations enhances collective defense efforts and enables organizations to stay informed about emerging threats. The more information SOC teams have about active threats, the better they can adapt their security strategies to mitigate risks.

Continuous monitoring also plays a critical role in regulatory compliance. Many cybersecurity regulations and industry standards, such as the General Data Protection Regulation (GDPR), the Payment Card Industry Data Security Standard (PCI DSS), and the National Institute of Standards and Technology (NIST) Cybersecurity Framework, require organizations to implement continuous monitoring practices. Compliance mandates often specify requirements for log retention, real-time threat detection, and incident reporting. By integrating continuous monitoring into their compliance strategies, organizations can meet regulatory requirements while improving their overall security posture.

Threat hunting is an essential component of continuous monitoring, allowing SOC analysts to proactively search for threats that may have bypassed automated detection systems. Threat hunters analyze security logs, network traffic, and system behavior to identify hidden threats and suspicious activities. By continuously refining threat hunting techniques based on new attack trends, SOC teams can improve their ability to detect and respond to sophisticated cyber threats. Threat hunting also enhances the effectiveness of continuous monitoring by identifying gaps in detection capabilities and providing insights for improving security analytics.

As cyber threats continue to evolve, organizations must adopt a mindset of continuous improvement in their security operations. Continuous monitoring and threat adaptation are not static processes but ongoing efforts that require constant refinement, automation, and intelligence-driven decision-making. By leveraging AI, automation, threat intelligence, and behavioral analytics, SOC teams can enhance their ability to detect and respond to threats in real time. The ability to continuously monitor and adapt to new threats is what separates a reactive security approach from a proactive and resilient cybersecurity strategy.

Handling Zero-Day Threats and Emerging Cyber Risks

Zero-day threats and emerging cyber risks present some of the most significant challenges for Security Operations Centers (SOCs). Unlike known vulnerabilities that have established patches and mitigation strategies, zero-day threats exploit previously unknown flaws in software, hardware, or network protocols. These vulnerabilities remain undetected by traditional security defenses until they are publicly disclosed or actively exploited by threat actors. The growing sophistication of cyber threats requires SOCs to adopt advanced detection, response, and mitigation strategies to address zero-day attacks and emerging cyber risks effectively.

Zero-day vulnerabilities can be exploited in multiple ways, including remote code execution, privilege escalation, data exfiltration, and malware injection. Attackers leverage these flaws to bypass security controls, infiltrate systems, and gain persistent access to an organization's infrastructure. Since no patches exist at the time of discovery, organizations must rely on proactive threat detection and mitigation techniques to reduce their exposure to such risks. Threat actors, including cybercriminal organizations, nation-state adversaries, and ransomware groups, actively seek and weaponize zero-day vulnerabilities before software vendors can develop security patches.

One of the primary challenges in handling zero-day threats is detection. Traditional security tools, such as signature-based antivirus software and intrusion detection systems (IDS), rely on known indicators of compromise (IOCs) to identify threats. However, zero-day attacks do not have existing signatures, making them difficult to detect using conventional methods. To counteract this, SOC teams must implement behavioral-based detection techniques, such as anomaly detection and heuristic analysis, to identify suspicious activity that deviates from normal system behavior.

Artificial intelligence (AI) and machine learning (ML) play a crucial role in identifying zero-day threats. AI-driven security analytics can analyze large volumes of security data to detect anomalies that may indicate an ongoing attack. By establishing baselines of normal system behavior, AI-powered solutions can identify deviations that suggest an exploit is occurring, even if the exact nature of the attack is unknown. Endpoint Detection and Response (EDR) and Network Detection and Response (NDR) solutions leverage AI to detect suspicious patterns, such as unusual file executions, unauthorized access attempts, or encrypted command-and-control (C2) communications.

Threat intelligence is another essential component of zero-day threat management. SOC teams must continuously gather and analyze threat intelligence from multiple sources, including open-source intelligence (OSINT), private threat intelligence platforms, and government cybersecurity agencies. Indicators of attack (IOAs), adversary tactics, techniques, and procedures (TTPs), and reports on newly discovered vulnerabilities help security teams anticipate potential threats. By integrating real-time threat intelligence feeds into their security monitoring tools, SOCs can detect early warning signs of zero-day attacks and take preventive measures before an exploit spreads.

Zero-day vulnerabilities often become public knowledge through responsible disclosure by security researchers or after they are exploited in the wild. When a zero-day vulnerability is disclosed, organizations must act quickly to assess their risk exposure and implement temporary mitigation strategies while waiting for an official patch from the software vendor. Virtual patching, a technique that involves deploying security controls at the network level to block exploit attempts, is a critical stopgap measure for protecting vulnerable systems. Web Application Firewalls (WAFs), Intrusion Prevention Systems (IPS), and behavioral analytics tools can help prevent exploitation by filtering out malicious traffic and detecting attempts to exploit known attack vectors.

Mitigating zero-day threats also requires a strong vulnerability management program. Organizations must conduct regular security assessments, penetration testing, and code reviews to identify weaknesses before attackers can exploit them. Secure software development practices, such as implementing secure coding standards, conducting regular security testing, and integrating automated vulnerability scanning into the development pipeline, help reduce the likelihood of introducing zero-day vulnerabilities into production environments. Applying the principle of least privilege (PoLP) and enforcing strict access controls further limit the impact of a potential exploit by restricting the attacker's ability to escalate privileges or move laterally within the network.

Incident response planning is critical for handling zero-day threats effectively. SOC teams must have predefined response playbooks that outline the steps to take when a zero-day vulnerability is identified. These playbooks should include processes for identifying affected systems, implementing temporary mitigations, and coordinating with software vendors for patch deployment. Security Orchestration, Automation, and Response (SOAR) platforms enhance incident response by automating containment actions, generating alerts, and initiating predefined remediation workflows.

Zero-day threats are often associated with emerging cyber risks, including advanced persistent threats (APTs), supply chain attacks, and nation-state cyber warfare. APT groups frequently exploit zero-day vulnerabilities as part of stealthy and long-term attack campaigns. These threats require SOC teams to continuously monitor for signs of compromise, such as unusual data exfiltration, persistence mechanisms, and unauthorized access to sensitive assets. Implementing a zero-trust security model, which enforces strict verification of all users and devices, reduces the attack surface and limits the ability of attackers to exploit zero-day vulnerabilities.

Supply chain attacks represent another emerging risk that exploits zero-day vulnerabilities. In these attacks, threat actors compromise trusted software vendors, cloud service providers, or third-party suppliers to distribute malware or gain unauthorized access to target organizations. The SolarWinds attack is a notable example of a supply chain compromise that leveraged a zero-day vulnerability to infiltrate multiple organizations worldwide. To mitigate the risk of supply chain attacks, organizations should implement strict third-party security assessments, require software vendors to follow secure development practices, and monitor software supply chains for anomalies.

Ransomware is also evolving to incorporate zero-day exploits into its attack strategies. Modern ransomware groups actively seek unpatched vulnerabilities to deploy ransomware payloads, encrypt critical data, and demand ransom payments. Defending against zero-day ransomware threats requires a multi-layered security approach, including endpoint security solutions, threat intelligence-driven detection, and robust backup strategies to enable quick recovery in the event of an attack.

Zero-day threats and emerging cyber risks demand continuous adaptation from SOC teams. Security analysts must stay updated on the latest cybersecurity trends, attend industry conferences, and participate in threat intelligence sharing communities. Organizations should conduct red teaming exercises to simulate real-world attacks and test their defenses against zero-day exploits. By continuously refining detection techniques, improving incident response processes, and staying ahead of adversary tactics, SOC teams can enhance their ability to handle zero-day threats and protect their organizations from the ever-evolving cyber threat landscape.

Crisis Management and Incident Escalation

Crisis management and incident escalation are fundamental components of an effective Security Operations Center (SOC). In the ever-evolving landscape of cyber threats, organizations must be prepared to handle security incidents that have the potential to disrupt operations, compromise sensitive data, and cause reputational damage. The ability to quickly identify, contain, and escalate incidents ensures that the right personnel and resources are allocated to mitigate threats before they escalate into full-blown crises. A well-structured crisis management and escalation process helps organizations minimize downtime, reduce financial losses, and maintain stakeholder confidence in their cybersecurity posture.

Crisis management in a SOC begins with a clear incident response framework that outlines how security events are detected, classified, and escalated based on their severity. Not all security incidents require the same level of response, so it is essential to establish predefined categories that help analysts prioritize threats. Low-severity incidents, such as failed login attempts or minor malware detections, can often be handled at the Tier 1 SOC level. However, high-severity incidents, such as a ransomware outbreak, data breach, or advanced persistent threat (APT) infiltration, require immediate escalation to senior security personnel, legal teams, and executive leadership.

Incident escalation is a structured process that ensures security threats receive the appropriate level of attention based on their impact and complexity. When an analyst identifies an anomaly or potential security breach, the first step is to assess the incident's severity and determine whether it requires further investigation. If an incident meets predefined escalation criteria, it must be reported to the next level of security personnel for deeper analysis and response. Escalation pathways must be clearly defined, ensuring that incidents are transferred to the appropriate teams without unnecessary delays. Effective escalation ensures that complex threats receive the attention of experienced security professionals who can analyze attack patterns, determine root causes, and implement containment strategies.

Communication is critical during a security crisis. SOC teams must have predefined communication channels and protocols to ensure that relevant stakeholders receive timely and accurate information. Internal communication between SOC analysts, incident responders, IT teams, and executive leadership must be structured to prevent confusion and misalignment. External communication is equally important, particularly when incidents involve regulatory reporting requirements or public disclosure obligations. Organizations must coordinate with legal teams, public relations specialists, and compliance officers to ensure that incident communication aligns with corporate policies and regulatory frameworks.

Real-time collaboration tools enhance crisis management efforts by enabling security teams to share threat intelligence, coordinate response actions, and track the status of an incident. Secure chat applications, ticketing systems, and automated alerting platforms ensure that all stakeholders remain informed and aligned on incident resolution efforts. Implementing a centralized incident response dashboard allows SOC teams to monitor incidents in real time, visualize attack trends, and assess the effectiveness of containment measures.

A well-defined incident response plan is a key component of effective crisis management. The plan should outline specific actions to be taken at each stage of an incident, from initial detection and analysis to containment, eradication, and recovery. Playbooks for different types of security incidents help SOC analysts respond consistently and efficiently to cyber threats. For example, a ransomware attack playbook may include immediate isolation of affected systems, backup restoration procedures, and notification steps for executive leadership. Regular testing and refinement of incident response playbooks ensure that security teams remain prepared for evolving cyber threats.

Crisis simulations and tabletop exercises help organizations assess their incident response readiness and identify gaps in their escalation procedures. These exercises simulate real-world attack scenarios, allowing SOC teams to practice their response actions in a controlled environment. By conducting crisis drills, organizations can evaluate their ability to detect threats, coordinate response efforts, and communicate effectively during an active incident. Lessons learned from these exercises help refine escalation protocols, improve coordination between security teams, and strengthen overall cybersecurity resilience.

Escalation thresholds should be regularly reviewed and updated to reflect the evolving threat landscape. As new attack vectors emerge, organizations must reassess their criteria for escalating incidents to higher levels of response. For example, an increase in targeted phishing attacks that bypass email security filters may warrant a change in escalation policies to ensure faster intervention by threat intelligence teams. Continuous improvement of escalation frameworks ensures that SOC teams remain agile and capable of addressing emerging cyber threats with precision.

Regulatory compliance plays a significant role in incident escalation, particularly for organizations operating in industries subject to strict cybersecurity regulations. Many compliance frameworks, such as the General Data Protection Regulation (GDPR), the Payment Card Industry Data Security Standard (PCI DSS), and the Health Insurance Portability and Accountability Act (HIPAA), require organizations to report security incidents within specific timeframes. Failure to comply with these reporting requirements can result in legal penalties and reputational damage. SOC teams must ensure that their incident escalation procedures align with regulatory mandates, enabling them to provide timely and accurate incident reports to regulatory authorities.

Incident containment and mitigation strategies vary depending on the nature of the security event. In some cases, immediate containment actions, such as blocking malicious IP addresses, isolating compromised endpoints, or revoking unauthorized user access, can prevent further damage. However, in large-scale attacks, containment efforts must be carefully coordinated to avoid disrupting critical business operations. SOC teams must work closely with IT and infrastructure teams to ensure that containment measures do not inadvertently impact legitimate users or essential services.

Post-incident analysis is a crucial aspect of crisis management. Once an incident has been resolved, SOC teams must conduct a thorough investigation to determine how the breach occurred, what security controls failed, and how similar incidents can be prevented in the future. A post-mortem review should include a detailed timeline of events, an assessment of response effectiveness, and recommendations for improving security defenses. Organizations should document their findings in an incident report, which serves as a valuable resource for refining incident response strategies and enhancing organizational resilience.

The integration of automation and artificial intelligence (AI) into incident escalation processes enhances efficiency and accuracy. AI-driven security analytics can help SOC teams prioritize incidents based on risk levels, reducing the manual workload on analysts. Automated response mechanisms, such as Security Orchestration, Automation, and Response (SOAR) platforms, streamline escalation workflows by assigning tasks to the appropriate teams, generating alerts, and triggering predefined response actions. By leveraging automation, SOC teams can improve response times and reduce the likelihood of human error during critical security events.

Crisis management and incident escalation require a proactive, structured approach that enables SOC teams to detect threats early, respond efficiently, and minimize the impact of security incidents. Organizations must establish clear escalation policies, define communication protocols, conduct regular crisis simulations, and continuously refine their incident response playbooks. By fostering a culture of preparedness, collaboration, and continuous improvement, SOC teams can enhance their ability to manage cybersecurity crises and protect organizations from the evolving threat landscape.

Communication and Collaboration in a SOC

Effective communication and collaboration are fundamental to the success of a Security Operations Center (SOC). Cyber threats evolve rapidly, and SOC teams must work together efficiently to detect, analyze, and respond to incidents in real time. Without clear communication channels and a structured approach to collaboration, security analysts, incident responders, and other stakeholders may struggle to coordinate their efforts, leading to delayed threat mitigation, increased operational risk, and potential security breaches. By fostering a culture of open communication, leveraging collaboration tools, and establishing well-defined processes, SOC teams can enhance their ability to protect an organization's digital assets.

A SOC is a high-pressure environment where multiple teams work simultaneously on various aspects of security monitoring, threat intelligence, and incident response. Analysts must continuously share findings, update colleagues on ongoing investigations, and escalate issues when necessary. To facilitate this, SOCs implement structured communication protocols that define how information should be shared within the team and across different departments. Standardized reporting formats, real-time notifications, and centralized dashboards help ensure that all team members have access to the latest threat intelligence and incident details.

One of the key aspects of effective SOC communication is the use of well-defined alerting and escalation mechanisms. Security Information and Event Management (SIEM) systems generate alerts based on detected anomalies, but without proper communication workflows, these alerts can be missed or improperly handled. SOC teams must establish clear guidelines on how alerts should be categorized, assigned, and escalated based on severity. Low-priority alerts may be addressed by Tier 1 analysts, while high-severity incidents require immediate attention from senior responders and may trigger executive notifications. Automated alerting systems integrated with messaging platforms help ensure that critical incidents receive the appropriate level of attention.

Collaboration between SOC teams and other departments within an organization is essential for a comprehensive security strategy. Cybersecurity is not solely the responsibility of SOC analysts; IT administrators, network engineers, compliance officers, legal teams, and executive leadership all play a role in maintaining a secure environment. When a security incident occurs, SOC teams must work closely with IT personnel to implement containment measures, forensic investigators to analyze compromised systems, and legal teams to ensure compliance with regulatory reporting requirements. Regular cross-departmental meetings, joint tabletop exercises, and incident response drills strengthen interdepartmental collaboration and improve overall security preparedness.

Threat intelligence sharing is another critical component of SOC collaboration. Cyber adversaries often target multiple organizations with similar attack techniques, and sharing intelligence about emerging threats can significantly enhance an organization's ability to defend itself. SOCs participate in threat intelligence-sharing communities, such as Information Sharing and Analysis Centers (ISACs) and industry-specific cybersecurity groups, to exchange information about attack patterns, indicators of compromise (IOCs), and adversary tactics. Integrating threat intelligence feeds into SOC workflows ensures that analysts stay informed about the latest threats and can proactively adjust their defenses accordingly.

Communication within a SOC is also dependent on the effective use of technology. Secure collaboration platforms, such as incident response management tools, dedicated SOC chat applications, and ticketing systems, enable seamless information sharing among team members. Real-time collaboration tools allow analysts to discuss active threats, document findings, and coordinate response actions efficiently. Automated documentation systems ensure that all incidents are recorded in a structured format, facilitating post-incident analysis and continuous improvement. By leveraging communication and collaboration technologies, SOC teams can streamline their workflows and enhance their incident response capabilities.

Security automation plays a vital role in improving SOC communication efficiency. Security Orchestration, Automation, and Response (SOAR) platforms integrate with SIEM systems, endpoint detection tools, and network security solutions to automate repetitive tasks and orchestrate response workflows. Automated playbooks guide SOC analysts through predefined incident response procedures, reducing the need for manual coordination and ensuring consistency in response actions. SOAR platforms also provide centralized dashboards where team members can track incident progress, assign tasks, and update investigation statuses in real time. By reducing the reliance on manual communication, automation enhances SOC efficiency and reduces response times.

Collaboration extends beyond internal SOC teams to external cybersecurity partners, vendors, and regulatory agencies. Many organizations rely on Managed Security Service Providers (MSSPs) or external cybersecurity consultants for threat analysis, incident response support, and forensic investigations. Establishing clear communication channels with external security partners ensures that information flows smoothly between in-house SOC teams and external specialists. When engaging third-party security providers, organizations must define service-level agreements (SLAs) that outline response expectations, reporting requirements, and escalation procedures to ensure a coordinated security effort.

Effective SOC communication also involves educating employees across the organization about cybersecurity risks and response protocols. Security awareness training ensures that employees understand how to report suspicious activities, recognize phishing attempts, and follow incident escalation procedures. Regular security briefings, newsletters, and simulated attack exercises keep employees informed about emerging threats and reinforce their role in the organization's cybersecurity posture. By fostering a culture of security awareness, SOC teams strengthen their organization's overall resilience against cyber threats.

Language barriers and global operations can pose communication challenges for multinational organizations with SOCs in different geographic regions. Organizations with global SOC operations must implement standardized communication protocols, adopt common security frameworks, and use multilingual security documentation to ensure effective coordination between regional teams. Time zone differences also require careful scheduling of shift handovers and incident reports to maintain continuous security coverage. Establishing a follow-the-sun SOC model, where security monitoring responsibilities are distributed across different time zones, helps organizations achieve 24/7 threat detection and response capabilities.

Crisis communication planning is a crucial aspect of SOC collaboration, particularly when dealing with major security incidents such as data breaches, ransomware attacks, or insider threats. Organizations must have predefined crisis communication plans that outline how information is disseminated internally and externally during a cyber crisis. Transparent and timely communication with executive leadership, legal teams, and regulatory bodies ensures that the organization responds effectively while maintaining compliance with reporting requirements. External communication with customers, stakeholders, and the media must be handled carefully to prevent misinformation and minimize reputational damage.

Continuous improvement in SOC communication and collaboration requires regular performance assessments and feedback loops. Conducting after-action reviews following major security incidents helps SOC teams evaluate the effectiveness of their communication strategies, identify areas for improvement, and implement lessons learned. Regular SOC maturity assessments, employee feedback surveys, and security operations audits provide valuable insights into communication strengths and weaknesses, allowing organizations to refine their collaborative processes.

Effective communication and collaboration are the backbone of a well-functioning SOC. By establishing clear communication protocols, leveraging advanced collaboration technologies, fostering interdepartmental cooperation, and engaging with external threat intelligence communities, SOC teams enhance their ability to detect, analyze, and respond to security threats. Strong communication practices ensure that all stakeholders are aligned, incidents are handled efficiently, and organizations remain resilient against evolving cyber risks.

Managing Third-Party Security Risks

Third-party security risks pose a significant challenge for organizations, as they rely on external vendors, service providers, and contractors to support business operations. While third parties provide essential services, they also introduce potential vulnerabilities that cybercriminals can exploit. Organizations must take a proactive approach to managing third-party security risks by implementing robust security policies, conducting continuous assessments, and ensuring compliance with regulatory requirements. A Security Operations Center (SOC) plays a critical role in monitoring, analyzing, and mitigating risks associated with third-party relationships to protect sensitive data and maintain operational resilience.

Third-party security risks arise when external entities have access to an organization's systems, networks, or sensitive information. These risks can manifest in various ways, including insecure data handling practices, poor access controls, software vulnerabilities, and supply chain attacks. Attackers often target third parties as an entry point to larger organizations, exploiting weaker security defenses to gain unauthorized access. The interconnected nature of modern business ecosystems makes it essential for organizations to continuously evaluate and strengthen the security posture of their third-party partners.

A comprehensive third-party risk management strategy begins with vendor assessment and due diligence. Before engaging with a third-party provider, organizations must evaluate its security practices, compliance with industry standards, and history of data breaches or security incidents. Vendors should be required to complete security questionnaires, provide audit reports, and demonstrate adherence to frameworks such as the National Institute of Standards and Technology (NIST) Cybersecurity Framework, ISO/IEC 27001, or the Payment Card Industry Data Security Standard (PCI DSS). Conducting background checks on vendors helps organizations identify potential risks before establishing formal business relationships.

Contractual agreements play a crucial role in defining security expectations between organizations and their third-party partners. Security clauses in contracts should outline data protection requirements, incident response procedures, compliance obligations, and liability for security breaches. Service Level Agreements (SLAs) should include specific cybersecurity expectations, such as encryption requirements, network monitoring responsibilities, and breach notification timelines. By establishing clear security obligations, organizations can ensure that third parties are held accountable for maintaining strong security controls.

Third-party access management is a key component of mitigating security risks. Organizations must enforce the principle of least privilege, ensuring that third-party vendors only have access to the systems and data necessary for their specific tasks. Privileged access should be strictly controlled, and organizations should implement multi-factor authentication (MFA) for all external users. Time-based and role-based access controls can help limit exposure by restricting access to sensitive systems based on job roles, project duration, or business needs. Continuous monitoring of third-party activities enables organizations to detect anomalies, unauthorized access attempts, and potential security breaches.

Regular security assessments and audits help organizations evaluate the effectiveness of third-party security controls. Organizations should conduct periodic penetration testing, vulnerability assessments, and compliance audits to identify weaknesses in third-party systems. Vendors should be required to participate in security assessments and demonstrate continuous improvement in their security posture. Third-party risk management platforms provide automated tools to assess vendor security ratings, track compliance with security policies, and monitor emerging threats related to external partners.

Supply chain security is an increasingly critical concern, as cybercriminals frequently target software vendors, hardware manufacturers, and cloud service providers to launch large-scale attacks. Organizations must ensure that third-party software and hardware providers follow secure development practices and conduct regular security testing. Software supply chain attacks, such as those involving malicious code injection or unauthorized software updates, can have devastating consequences. Implementing strict software validation processes, code signing mechanisms, and integrity checks helps organizations protect against compromised third-party software.

Incident response planning is essential for mitigating the impact of third-party security breaches. Organizations must have predefined procedures for handling security incidents involving third parties, including breach containment, forensic investigation, and communication with affected stakeholders. Third-party vendors should be required to report security incidents promptly and cooperate with incident response teams to resolve issues. Organizations should establish joint incident response exercises with key third-party providers to ensure coordinated and effective threat mitigation efforts.

Cyber threat intelligence integration enhances an organization's ability to detect and respond to third-party security risks. SOC teams should actively monitor threat intelligence feeds for indicators of compromise (IOCs) related to third-party vendors, emerging attack techniques, and known vulnerabilities in third-party software. Sharing threat intelligence with trusted partners and industry peers can help organizations stay ahead of potential threats. By incorporating real-time threat intelligence into security monitoring tools, organizations can quickly identify and neutralize risks associated with third-party connections.

Compliance with regulatory requirements is another critical aspect of third-party security risk management. Many industries are subject to cybersecurity regulations that require organizations to ensure the security of third-party vendors. Regulations such as the General Data Protection Regulation (GDPR), the Health Insurance Portability and Accountability Act (HIPAA), and the Federal Risk and Authorization Management Program (FedRAMP) mandate strict third-party security controls. Organizations must conduct regular compliance audits, maintain documentation of third-party security measures, and establish reporting mechanisms to demonstrate adherence to regulatory standards.

Data protection is a top priority when managing third-party security risks. Organizations must ensure that third parties follow strict data handling policies, including data encryption, secure storage, and controlled data sharing. Data loss prevention (DLP) solutions help monitor and prevent unauthorized data transfers by third-party vendors. Tokenization and anonymization techniques can further reduce the risk of sensitive data exposure by ensuring that third parties only have access to anonymized or encrypted datasets.

Employee training and awareness programs play a vital role in managing third-party security risks. Organizations must educate employees on the risks associated with third-party vendors and provide guidance on securely interacting with external partners. Security awareness training should cover topics such as phishing attacks targeting third-party relationships, secure file sharing practices, and reporting suspicious activities related to vendor access. Ensuring that employees understand the potential threats associated with third-party interactions strengthens the organization's overall security posture.

Continuous improvement is essential in third-party security risk management. As cyber threats evolve, organizations must regularly reassess their third-party security strategies, update security policies, and implement new technologies to enhance visibility and control. Establishing a dedicated third-party risk management team within the SOC ensures that third-party security concerns receive ongoing attention. Organizations should also collaborate with vendors to improve security practices, share best practices, and jointly develop strategies to mitigate emerging threats.

Managing third-party security risks requires a proactive approach that includes comprehensive vendor assessments, strong contractual agreements, strict access controls, continuous monitoring, and robust incident response planning. By integrating security best practices into third-party relationships, organizations can reduce their exposure to cyber threats, protect sensitive data, and maintain trust with customers and stakeholders. A well-structured third-party security risk management program enhances an organization's ability to navigate the complex and interconnected cybersecurity landscape while maintaining operational resilience.

Establishing a Threat Intelligence Sharing Program

A threat intelligence sharing program is a crucial component of modern cybersecurity strategies, enabling organizations to enhance their ability to detect, prevent, and respond to cyber threats. Security Operations Centers (SOCs) benefit significantly from threat intelligence sharing, as it provides real-time insights into emerging attack vectors, malicious actors, and vulnerabilities affecting industries worldwide. By participating in structured intelligence-sharing initiatives, organizations gain a broader understanding of the evolving threat landscape and can proactively strengthen their defenses. Establishing an effective threat intelligence sharing program requires careful planning, collaboration with trusted partners, and the integration of threat intelligence into security operations.

Threat intelligence sharing involves collecting, analyzing, and disseminating cyber threat information between organizations, industry groups, government agencies, and cybersecurity vendors. This exchange of intelligence helps security teams stay ahead of cyber adversaries by identifying attack patterns, indicators of compromise (IOCs), and tactics, techniques, and procedures (TTPs) used by malicious actors. Organizations that operate in isolation are at a disadvantage, as they may only detect threats after experiencing an attack. By contrast, those that participate in threat intelligence sharing can anticipate and mitigate risks before they materialize.

One of the first steps in establishing a threat intelligence sharing program is defining the objectives and scope of intelligence exchange. Organizations must determine what types of intelligence they will share, who the recipients will be, and how frequently the information will be updated. Threat intelligence can include indicators such as malicious IP addresses, domain names, file hashes, phishing campaigns, malware signatures, and behavioral threat patterns. Additionally, organizations may share strategic intelligence, including threat actor profiles, attack motives, and geopolitical cybersecurity risks. Clearly defining the scope of intelligence sharing ensures that the program aligns with organizational security goals and compliance requirements.

Participation in threat intelligence sharing programs requires collaboration with trusted partners, industry groups, and governmental cybersecurity organizations. Many industries have established Information Sharing and Analysis Centers (ISACs) that facilitate threat intelligence exchange among companies facing similar risks. ISACs exist for financial services, healthcare, energy, and other critical sectors, providing a secure platform for sharing intelligence about industry-specific threats. Government-backed initiatives, such as the Cybersecurity and Infrastructure Security Agency (CISA) in the United States and the European Union Agency for Cybersecurity

(ENISA), also promote intelligence sharing between private organizations and public-sector entities.

Integrating automated threat intelligence feeds into security operations enhances the efficiency of a SOC. Threat intelligence platforms (TIPs) aggregate data from multiple sources, normalize the information, and provide actionable insights for security teams. By leveraging automated intelligence feeds, SOC analysts can enrich security alerts with contextual information, prioritize high-risk threats, and refine detection rules in Security Information and Event Management (SIEM) systems. Automated threat intelligence sharing reduces the time required to analyze threats manually and enables organizations to respond to cyber incidents with greater speed and accuracy.

Security teams must ensure that shared threat intelligence is actionable and relevant to their organization's security needs. Raw data without context can lead to information overload, making it difficult for analysts to distinguish between critical threats and false positives. Effective intelligence-sharing programs focus on providing contextualized information, including the likelihood of exploitation, attack vectors used, and recommended mitigation strategies. SOC teams should establish processes to validate incoming intelligence, filter out irrelevant data, and correlate shared information with internal security events. By refining intelligence-sharing workflows, organizations can maximize the value of shared threat intelligence.

Legal and compliance considerations are critical when establishing a threat intelligence sharing program. Organizations must ensure that shared intelligence does not violate data protection laws, confidentiality agreements, or industry regulations. Regulations such as the General Data Protection Regulation (GDPR) impose strict requirements on handling personally identifiable information (PII), making it necessary to anonymize or redact sensitive data before sharing. Legal teams should be involved in the development of intelligence-sharing agreements, ensuring that data-sharing practices align with corporate policies and regulatory mandates. Establishing a legal framework for threat intelligence sharing reduces the risk of liability while enabling secure collaboration between organizations.

Cyber threat intelligence sharing programs also benefit from a structured framework that defines roles, responsibilities, and escalation procedures. Security teams should assign dedicated personnel responsible for managing intelligence collection, validation, and dissemination. Establishing formal intelligence-sharing agreements (ISAs) or memorandums of understanding (MOUs) with trusted partners sets clear expectations regarding the use, storage, and distribution of shared intelligence. SOCs should also implement security controls to protect intelligence-sharing platforms from unauthorized access, ensuring that sensitive threat data remains secure.

A successful threat intelligence sharing program must include mechanisms for measuring effectiveness and continuous improvement. Organizations should track key performance indicators (KPIs) such as the number of threat indicators shared, the percentage of shared intelligence used in incident response, and the reduction in dwell time for detected threats. Conducting regular assessments of intelligence-sharing practices helps organizations refine their approach, identify gaps, and enhance collaboration with partners. Threat intelligence sharing is an ongoing process that evolves based on emerging cyber threats and lessons learned from past incidents.

Collaboration between private organizations, public agencies, and cybersecurity researchers strengthens global cyber defense efforts. By participating in intelligence-sharing communities, organizations contribute to a collective security posture that benefits the entire industry. Adversaries operate across borders and often use similar attack techniques against multiple targets. Sharing intelligence about these threats helps disrupt cybercriminal operations, improve global threat visibility, and create a more resilient cybersecurity ecosystem. SOC teams that actively engage in intelligence-sharing initiatives gain access to valuable threat data that enhances their ability to defend against sophisticated cyber attacks.

Threat intelligence sharing also fosters a culture of trust and cooperation among cybersecurity professionals. Organizations that share intelligence openly and responsibly build strong relationships with industry peers, enabling faster response to emerging threats. Collaborative security efforts reduce the burden on individual SOC teams by distributing threat intelligence across a network of trusted partners. As cyber threats continue to grow in complexity, fostering a culture of information exchange ensures that organizations remain ahead of attackers and better equipped to mitigate cyber risks.

Establishing a threat intelligence sharing program enhances a SOC's ability to anticipate, detect, and respond to cyber threats with greater efficiency. By defining clear objectives, integrating automated intelligence feeds, collaborating with trusted partners, ensuring legal compliance, and continuously refining intelligence-sharing practices, organizations can strengthen their security posture. Participation in threat intelligence exchange initiatives contributes to a more resilient cybersecurity ecosystem, enabling organizations to stay ahead of adversaries and protect critical assets from evolving cyber threats.

The Role of Cyber Threat Emulation in a SOC

Cyber threat emulation is a critical practice within a Security Operations Center (SOC) that enables security teams to test their defenses against real-world attack scenarios. Unlike traditional penetration testing, which focuses on identifying vulnerabilities, cyber threat emulation replicates the tactics, techniques, and procedures (TTPs) used by adversaries to evaluate an organization's ability to detect, respond to, and mitigate cyber threats. By simulating actual attack behaviors, SOC analysts can assess the effectiveness of security controls, refine incident response strategies, and strengthen the overall security posture of the organization.

The primary objective of cyber threat emulation is to simulate how real attackers operate within an environment. This includes testing an organization's ability to identify early indicators of compromise, detect lateral movement, respond to privilege escalation attempts, and contain potential breaches. By mimicking adversarial behavior, SOC teams can uncover gaps in their security infrastructure, improve detection capabilities, and refine response playbooks. Cyber threat emulation also helps organizations assess whether their security investments are effective in preventing advanced attacks.

One of the most widely used frameworks for cyber threat emulation is the MITRE ATT&CK framework. This knowledge base provides a detailed classification of known attack techniques used by cyber adversaries, allowing SOC teams to create realistic attack scenarios that align with actual threats. By mapping attack simulations to the MITRE ATT&CK framework, organizations can systematically test their defenses against specific tactics such as credential dumping, persistence mechanisms, and data exfiltration. This structured approach ensures that threat emulation exercises are aligned with real-world threat intelligence and reflect the latest attack trends.

Red teaming is a key component of cyber threat emulation, involving dedicated security professionals who act as adversaries to challenge an organization's defenses. Unlike traditional vulnerability assessments, red teams conduct stealthy, goal-oriented attack simulations to test the resilience of a SOC's monitoring and detection capabilities. Red team exercises often include spear-phishing attacks, exploitation of misconfigured systems, and attempts to bypass endpoint security controls. These simulations provide valuable insights into how attackers may evade detection and compromise critical assets.

Purple teaming enhances cyber threat emulation by fostering collaboration between offensive (red team) and defensive (blue team) security professionals. Instead of working in isolation, both teams share insights and findings in real time to improve detection and response capabilities. During a purple team exercise, red team operators simulate an attack, while blue team analysts monitor for signs of compromise and refine detection mechanisms. This iterative approach allows SOC teams to enhance threat visibility, optimize security tool configurations, and develop more effective incident response procedures.

Automated adversary emulation platforms further enhance cyber threat emulation by replicating real-world attacks in a controlled environment. These platforms enable SOC teams to execute predefined attack scenarios, measure detection performance, and validate security controls without requiring manual red teaming.

Automated threat emulation tools integrate with Security Information and Event Management (SIEM) systems, Endpoint Detection and Response (EDR) solutions, and Security Orchestration, Automation, and Response (SOAR) platforms to provide continuous validation of security effectiveness. By using automated adversary emulation, organizations can conduct frequent testing and ensure that their security posture remains resilient against evolving threats.

One of the key benefits of cyber threat emulation is its ability to enhance threat hunting capabilities within a SOC. Threat hunters rely on advanced detection techniques to proactively identify hidden threats that may have bypassed traditional security controls. By emulating sophisticated attack behaviors, SOC teams can develop new detection signatures, refine log analysis techniques, and improve anomaly detection models. Threat emulation also helps validate the effectiveness of threat intelligence integration by testing whether SOC analysts can correlate attack indicators with known adversary behaviors.

Cyber threat emulation plays a crucial role in validating incident response processes. Organizations must ensure that their SOC teams can effectively contain and remediate cyber threats when an attack occurs. Threat emulation exercises help security teams test their response times, evaluate escalation procedures, and improve coordination between different departments. By conducting regular incident response drills based on threat emulation scenarios, organizations can enhance their ability to handle real security incidents with greater speed and efficiency.

Regulatory compliance and industry standards increasingly emphasize the importance of proactive security testing, including cyber threat emulation. Compliance frameworks such as the National Institute of Standards and Technology (NIST) Cybersecurity Framework, ISO/IEC 27001, and the Payment Card Industry Data Security Standard (PCI DSS) recommend continuous security validation as part of a comprehensive cybersecurity strategy. Organizations that conduct regular cyber threat emulation exercises can demonstrate their commitment to security best practices, improve audit readiness, and ensure compliance with regulatory requirements.

SOC teams must also integrate cyber threat emulation with business continuity planning. Cyberattacks have the potential to disrupt critical operations, and organizations must be prepared to recover quickly in the event of a breach. By simulating ransomware attacks, supply chain compromises, and insider threats, SOC teams can assess the impact of security incidents on business functions and refine their disaster recovery strategies. Threat emulation helps organizations identify weaknesses in backup procedures, incident escalation protocols, and crisis communication plans, ensuring that they can maintain business continuity during a cyber crisis.

Continuous improvement is essential in cyber threat emulation. SOC teams must analyze the results of each emulation exercise, document lessons learned, and implement security enhancements based on findings. Threat actors constantly evolve their attack techniques, requiring organizations to adapt their security defenses accordingly. By maintaining an ongoing cycle of testing, refinement, and adaptation, SOC teams can stay ahead of adversaries and strengthen their overall cybersecurity resilience.

As cyber threats grow in sophistication, organizations must adopt proactive security measures to defend against emerging attack techniques. Cyber threat emulation provides SOC teams with a powerful tool to assess their security posture, enhance threat detection capabilities, and improve incident response effectiveness. By integrating threat emulation into daily security operations, collaborating across red and blue teams, and leveraging automated adversary simulation platforms, organizations can create a robust defense strategy that prepares them for real-world cyber threats.

SOC Governance and Policy Development

Security Operations Center (SOC) governance and policy development are essential for ensuring that cybersecurity operations align with an organization's overall security strategy, compliance requirements, and risk management objectives. Governance establishes the framework within which the SOC operates, defining roles, responsibilities, reporting structures, and decision-making processes. Policies serve as the foundation for SOC activities, guiding analysts, security engineers, and incident responders in handling security threats effectively. Without well-defined governance and policies, a SOC may struggle with inefficiencies, unclear accountability, and inconsistent security practices.

SOC governance begins with defining the overall mission and objectives of the security operations team. Organizations must determine whether the SOC will operate as an internal function, an outsourced service through a Managed Security Service Provider (MSSP), or a hybrid model that combines in-house and external security resources. The governance framework should align with the organization's broader cybersecurity strategy, ensuring that the SOC's priorities support business continuity, regulatory compliance, and risk management initiatives. Clearly documented governance structures provide clarity on how security incidents are escalated, who has decision-making authority, and how security policies evolve over time.

Roles and responsibilities within the SOC must be clearly outlined to avoid confusion and overlap. SOC analysts, threat hunters, security engineers, and incident response teams must understand their specific duties and how they contribute to the organization's cybersecurity posture. Tiered SOC structures, often organized into Level 1, Level 2, and Level 3 analysts, help ensure that security alerts are escalated appropriately based on their severity. Additionally, the governance framework should define the relationships between the SOC and other teams, such as IT, legal, compliance, and executive leadership. Collaboration between these groups ensures a coordinated response to security threats and aligns SOC activities with business objectives.

SOC policies serve as formal guidelines that define how security monitoring, incident response, threat intelligence, and reporting are conducted. These policies must be comprehensive, covering areas such as log management, access controls, data retention, vulnerability management, and security awareness training. Each policy must outline specific procedures, enforcement mechanisms, and accountability measures to ensure consistent security operations. Organizations should regularly review and update SOC policies to reflect emerging cyber threats, evolving regulatory requirements, and changes in business operations.

Incident response policies are a critical aspect of SOC governance. These policies define the procedures for detecting, analyzing, containing, eradicating, and recovering from security incidents. The policy should specify how incidents are classified based on their severity, who is responsible for responding to different types of threats, and how communication is managed during an active incident. Incident response playbooks should accompany these policies, providing SOC analysts with step-by-step guidance on responding to various attack scenarios, such as ransomware infections, insider threats, and Distributed Denial of Service (DDoS) attacks.

Access control policies within the SOC help regulate who can access sensitive systems and data. A least privilege model ensures that SOC personnel only have the permissions necessary to perform their job functions, reducing the risk of insider threats and accidental security breaches. Multi-factor authentication (MFA), role-based access control (RBAC), and continuous monitoring of privileged accounts help enforce access control policies. Organizations should conduct periodic access reviews to verify that users retain appropriate permissions and revoke access for individuals who no longer require it.

Log management and data retention policies govern how security logs are collected, stored, and analyzed within the SOC. Effective log management ensures that security analysts have the necessary visibility to detect and investigate security threats. Organizations must define which logs are collected from firewalls, endpoint security tools, network devices, and cloud environments. Retention policies should specify how long logs are stored, taking into account regulatory requirements such as the General Data Protection Regulation (GDPR), the Health Insurance Portability and Accountability Act (HIPAA), and the Payment Card Industry Data Security Standard (PCI DSS). Proper log retention helps SOC teams conduct forensic investigations, identify attack patterns, and meet compliance obligations.

Threat intelligence policies outline how the SOC collects, processes, and shares information about emerging cyber threats. These policies should define which threat intelligence sources the organization relies on, how intelligence feeds are integrated into security monitoring systems, and how threat intelligence is disseminated to relevant stakeholders. Threat intelligence-sharing agreements with industry groups, government agencies, and cybersecurity vendors must be established to enhance the SOC's ability to anticipate and mitigate threats. Security teams should regularly validate threat intelligence sources to ensure the accuracy and relevance of the data used for threat detection.

Compliance and regulatory policies ensure that SOC operations adhere to legal and industry-specific cybersecurity requirements. Organizations must define which regulatory frameworks apply to their operations and establish policies that align with these requirements. Security audits, risk assessments, and compliance reviews help SOC teams identify gaps in security controls and implement corrective actions. Compliance policies should also outline reporting requirements for security incidents, specifying when and how organizations must notify regulatory authorities, customers, and business partners about data breaches or cyberattacks.

Metrics and key performance indicators (KPIs) help measure the effectiveness of SOC governance and policy enforcement. Organizations should establish metrics that track the efficiency of threat detection, incident response times, false positive rates, and security control effectiveness. Regular reporting on these metrics allows leadership to assess SOC performance, allocate resources effectively, and refine security policies as needed. SOC governance frameworks should include continuous improvement mechanisms that ensure policies evolve based on lessons learned from past incidents and advancements in cybersecurity technology.

Training and awareness policies are necessary to ensure that SOC personnel remain up to date with the latest security threats, attack techniques, and best practices. SOC teams should participate in ongoing cybersecurity training programs, attend industry conferences, and engage in hands-on exercises such as red teaming and threat hunting simulations. Organizations should also implement security awareness programs for non-SOC employees, educating staff on phishing threats, password security, and secure data handling practices. Well-trained employees strengthen the organization's security posture by reducing human-related security risks.

Collaboration and coordination policies define how the SOC interacts with external cybersecurity partners, law enforcement agencies, and third-party security service providers. In cases where an organization outsources SOC functions to a managed security services provider (MSSP), governance policies must specify service level agreements (SLAs), reporting expectations, and escalation procedures. Establishing clear guidelines for external collaboration ensures that security incidents are handled efficiently and in compliance with legal and contractual obligations.

Regular policy reviews and governance audits help ensure that SOC operations remain aligned with the organization's evolving security needs. Cyber threats continuously change, requiring organizations to adapt their security policies to address new risks. SOC teams should conduct annual policy reviews, solicit feedback from stakeholders, and update governance frameworks to reflect emerging best practices. Keeping policies current ensures that security operations remain effective in protecting the organization from evolving cyber threats.

SOC governance and policy development provide the foundation for a well-structured, efficient, and resilient security operations function. By establishing clear roles, responsibilities, and security policies, organizations can ensure that their SOC operates effectively, maintains compliance with industry regulations, and adapts to the evolving cybersecurity landscape. Well-defined governance structures and policies empower SOC teams to detect, respond to, and mitigate threats with greater efficiency, ultimately strengthening the organization's overall security posture.

Evaluating and Choosing Security Tools for Your SOC

Selecting the right security tools for a Security Operations Center (SOC) is a critical decision that directly impacts an organization's ability to detect, respond to, and mitigate cyber threats. With the increasing complexity of cyberattacks, SOC teams must be equipped with tools that provide comprehensive visibility, advanced analytics, and automation capabilities. The evaluation and selection process requires careful consideration of organizational needs, security objectives, compliance requirements, and the existing IT infrastructure. An effective SOC relies on an integrated ecosystem of security technologies that work together seamlessly to enhance threat detection and response capabilities.

The first step in evaluating security tools for a SOC is defining the organization's security requirements and operational goals. Different industries face varying cyber threats, regulatory requirements, and risk profiles, which influence the selection of security technologies. Organizations must assess their security priorities, whether they focus on threat intelligence, real-time monitoring, incident response, or compliance enforcement. Conducting a risk assessment helps SOC teams identify gaps in their current security posture and determine which tools are necessary to strengthen their defenses.

A core component of any SOC is a Security Information and Event Management (SIEM) system, which collects, correlates, and analyzes security data from multiple sources. SIEM solutions provide real-time visibility into security events, enabling SOC analysts to detect anomalies, investigate incidents, and generate reports for compliance purposes. When evaluating SIEM platforms, organizations should consider factors such as scalability, integration capabilities, log storage capacity, and threat intelligence integration. Advanced SIEM solutions incorporate machine learning and behavioral analytics to enhance threat detection by identifying deviations from normal activity patterns.

Another essential tool for a SOC is Endpoint Detection and Response (EDR), which provides deep visibility into endpoint activities and detects malicious behaviors on workstations, servers, and mobile devices. EDR solutions continuously monitor endpoints for signs of compromise, such as unauthorized process executions, file modifications, and unusual network connections. Organizations should evaluate EDR tools based on their ability to provide real-time alerts, forensic investigation features, and automated response capabilities. Some advanced EDR platforms integrate with threat intelligence feeds to enhance detection accuracy and reduce false positives.

Network Detection and Response (NDR) solutions complement EDR by monitoring network traffic for indicators of compromise (IOCs) and suspicious behaviors. NDR tools analyze packet data, detect lateral movement, and identify command-and-control (C2) communications used by threat actors. These solutions leverage artificial intelligence and anomaly detection to identify stealthy attacks that bypass traditional security controls. When selecting an NDR solution, SOC teams should consider its ability to detect encrypted threats, analyze east-west network traffic, and integrate with other security tools.

To enhance threat intelligence capabilities, organizations should invest in Threat Intelligence Platforms (TIPs) that aggregate and analyze threat data from multiple sources. TIPs provide SOC analysts with contextualized intelligence about emerging cyber threats, attack methodologies, and known adversary tactics. By integrating TIPs with SIEM, EDR, and NDR solutions, SOC teams can enrich security alerts with relevant threat intelligence, improving incident response efficiency. Organizations should evaluate TIPs based on their ability to provide actionable intelligence, automate threat enrichment, and support threat intelligence sharing with industry peers.

Security Orchestration, Automation, and Response (SOAR) platforms streamline SOC operations by automating repetitive tasks, orchestrating response workflows, and integrating security tools into a unified ecosystem. SOAR platforms enable SOC teams to automate alert triage, initiate incident response actions, and improve collaboration between security analysts. Organizations should assess SOAR solutions based on their playbook customization capabilities, integration with existing security infrastructure, and ability to facilitate threat hunting and forensic investigations.

In cloud-based environments, Cloud Security Posture Management (CSPM) and Cloud Workload Protection Platforms (CWPP) help SOC teams secure cloud assets, detect misconfigurations, and enforce security policies. As organizations migrate workloads to cloud environments, securing cloud resources becomes a top priority. CSPM tools continuously scan cloud environments for security risks, while CWPP solutions monitor cloud workloads for threats and unauthorized activities. Organizations should choose cloud security tools that provide visibility across multi-cloud environments, enforce compliance policies, and integrate with SOC workflows.

Vulnerability management tools are also essential for proactive security defense. Vulnerability Assessment and Patch Management solutions help organizations identify and remediate security weaknesses in software, applications, and infrastructure. These tools provide continuous scanning, risk-based prioritization, and automated patch deployment to reduce exposure to known vulnerabilities. SOC teams should evaluate vulnerability management tools based on their ability to provide real-time risk assessments, integrate with SIEM platforms, and automate remediation workflows.

Deception technologies add an extra layer of defense by deploying honeypots, decoy systems, and fake credentials to lure and detect attackers. These tools provide valuable intelligence on attacker tactics and help SOC teams identify potential threats before they cause significant damage. Organizations should consider deception technology solutions that seamlessly integrate with existing security infrastructure and provide in-depth threat analytics.

The integration and interoperability of security tools play a critical role in the effectiveness of a SOC. A fragmented security stack with disconnected tools can lead to inefficiencies, data silos, and increased response times. Organizations should prioritize security solutions that support open APIs, standardized data formats, and seamless integrations with existing security infrastructure. Centralized visibility and cross-platform correlation enhance the SOC's ability to detect and respond to threats in real time.

When evaluating security tools, organizations should also consider ease of use, deployment flexibility, and scalability. A complex or difficult-to-manage security tool can increase the burden on SOC analysts and reduce operational efficiency. User-friendly interfaces, intuitive dashboards, and automation features improve the productivity of SOC teams. Additionally, organizations should ensure that their chosen security tools can scale with growing data volumes, evolving threats, and expanding IT environments.

Cost considerations are another important factor in selecting security tools. Organizations must balance their security budget with the need for effective threat detection and response capabilities. Total cost of ownership (TCO) should be evaluated, including licensing fees, maintenance costs, and personnel training requirements. While investing in advanced security tools is necessary, organizations should prioritize solutions that provide measurable value, reduce operational complexity, and enhance overall security posture.

Testing and proof-of-concept (PoC) evaluations allow organizations to assess security tools before making final purchasing decisions. Running a PoC in a controlled environment helps SOC teams determine how well a tool integrates with existing workflows, how effectively it detects threats, and whether it meets performance expectations. Engaging security vendors in demonstrations, conducting hands-on testing, and collecting feedback from SOC analysts ensure that the selected tools align with the organization's security needs.

Choosing the right security tools for a SOC requires a strategic and systematic approach. By assessing security needs, prioritizing integration, leveraging automation, and ensuring ease of use, organizations can build a robust security operations framework. Investing in the right technologies enhances threat detection, improves response efficiency, and strengthens an organization's ability to defend against evolving cyber threats.

Conducting Red Team Assessments for SOC Improvement

Red team assessments play a crucial role in strengthening the effectiveness of a Security Operations Center (SOC) by simulating real-world cyberattacks to test the organization's detection, response, and mitigation capabilities. Unlike traditional penetration testing, which primarily focuses on identifying technical vulnerabilities, red team exercises evaluate the overall security posture, including the ability of security analysts to detect and respond to sophisticated attack scenarios. By conducting controlled adversarial simulations, organizations can identify weaknesses in security monitoring, refine incident response procedures, and enhance overall cyber resilience.

The goal of a red team assessment is to mimic the tactics, techniques, and procedures (TTPs) used by real-world adversaries, including cybercriminal groups, nation-state actors, and insider threats. Red teams operate covertly, attempting to infiltrate the organization's infrastructure without being detected by security controls or SOC personnel. This approach provides valuable insights into the effectiveness of existing security measures, allowing SOC teams to fine-tune their threat detection and incident response capabilities. The insights gained from red team assessments help organizations implement targeted security improvements that address both technical and procedural gaps.

A successful red team exercise requires careful planning and coordination. Before launching an assessment, the red team and key stakeholders must define the objectives, scope, and rules of engagement. The scope determines which systems, networks, and applications will be tested, while the rules of engagement establish boundaries to ensure that operations do not disrupt critical business functions. The red team must work closely with executive leadership and legal teams to ensure that the assessment aligns with compliance requirements and ethical hacking standards.

One of the key aspects of red team assessments is reconnaissance, where red team members gather intelligence about the target organization. This phase involves open-source intelligence (OSINT) gathering, social engineering, network enumeration, and analysis of publicly available information. By simulating how real attackers conduct reconnaissance, red teams can identify exposed assets, weak credentials, and misconfigurations that could be exploited in an attack. The intelligence collected during this phase helps the red team develop a realistic attack strategy that closely resembles real-world threats.

After reconnaissance, the red team attempts to gain initial access to the organization's network. This can be achieved through phishing campaigns, exploiting known vulnerabilities, or bypassing weak authentication controls. The ability of the SOC to detect and respond to these activities is a critical measure of its effectiveness. If the red team successfully gains access, they proceed with privilege escalation techniques, moving laterally within the network, exfiltrating data, or establishing persistence. These tactics help test the organization's endpoint detection and response (EDR) capabilities, log correlation accuracy, and behavioral analytics efficiency.

Throughout the assessment, the SOC's ability to detect and investigate malicious activities is continuously evaluated. A well-prepared SOC should have the visibility and monitoring capabilities necessary to identify anomalies, flag unauthorized access attempts, and escalate potential security incidents. If the red team remains undetected, it may indicate that detection rules, security tools, or SOC workflows need improvement. Even if some activities are detected, delays in response time or misinterpretation of attack patterns can highlight areas where SOC analysts require additional training or automation enhancements.

One of the most valuable aspects of red team assessments is the post-engagement debriefing. Once the assessment is complete, the red team shares detailed findings with the SOC and security leadership. The debriefing includes an analysis of successful attack paths, security gaps, and missed detection opportunities. SOC teams review logs, alerts, and incident reports to understand what was detected, what was overlooked, and how responses could have been improved. This collaborative evaluation helps transform the findings into actionable security enhancements, allowing the organization to refine its defenses against future attacks.

Purple teaming is an effective approach that combines red team assessments with defensive collaboration. Unlike traditional red teaming, where the blue team (SOC) is unaware of the attack scenarios, purple teaming involves continuous communication between red and blue teams. This approach allows SOC analysts to observe attack tactics in real time, adjust detection rules, and test response strategies as the red team operates. By fostering direct collaboration, purple teaming accelerates security improvements and enhances the SOC's ability to recognize evolving threats.

Automated adversary emulation platforms complement red team assessments by allowing organizations to conduct continuous security validation without requiring a dedicated red team. These platforms use prebuilt attack scenarios based on frameworks like MITRE ATT&CK to simulate real-world threats and measure detection effectiveness. By integrating automated red teaming tools with Security Information and Event Management (SIEM) systems, Endpoint Detection and Response (EDR) solutions, and Security Orchestration, Automation, and Response (SOAR) platforms, organizations can continuously assess and improve their security posture.

Red team assessments also provide valuable insights into security awareness training effectiveness. Many attacks exploit human vulnerabilities, such as phishing, social engineering, and credential reuse. If employees frequently fall victim to simulated phishing attempts or fail to report suspicious activities, it indicates the need for improved security awareness programs. By analyzing red team findings, organizations can tailor their training efforts to address specific weaknesses and reinforce cybersecurity best practices across all employees.

Regulatory compliance and industry standards increasingly emphasize the importance of proactive security testing, including red team exercises. Frameworks such as the National Institute of Standards and Technology (NIST) Cybersecurity Framework, ISO/IEC 27001, and the Payment Card Industry Data Security Standard (PCI DSS) recommend continuous security validation as part of a comprehensive cybersecurity strategy. By conducting regular red team assessments, organizations can demonstrate compliance, improve audit readiness, and strengthen their cybersecurity defenses against sophisticated threats.

Red team assessments should not be a one-time exercise but rather an ongoing process integrated into the organization's cybersecurity strategy. Cyber threats continuously evolve, and security defenses must adapt accordingly. By conducting periodic red team engagements, organizations ensure that their SOC remains agile, proactive, and capable of handling emerging attack techniques. Continuous improvement based on red team findings helps organizations stay ahead of adversaries and maintain a strong security posture.

By leveraging red team assessments, organizations gain a deeper understanding of their security strengths and weaknesses. These exercises provide valuable insights that help SOC teams refine their detection capabilities, enhance incident response workflows, and strengthen overall cyber resilience. Whether conducted internally, through external red teaming engagements, or with automated adversary emulation tools, red team assessments serve as an essential component of a proactive cybersecurity strategy, ensuring that organizations are prepared to defend against real-world threats.

Lessons Learned from Real-World SOC Incidents

Security Operations Centers (SOCs) play a vital role in defending organizations against cyber threats, but even the most well-equipped SOCs encounter incidents that expose vulnerabilities, inefficiencies, and gaps in security controls. Real-world incidents provide invaluable lessons that help organizations refine their security strategies, improve response times, and strengthen their overall resilience against cyberattacks. By analyzing these incidents, SOC teams can identify common challenges, optimize detection mechanisms, and enhance collaboration between security, IT, and executive leadership. Every breach, attempted intrusion, or security misconfiguration offers an opportunity for growth and refinement of security operations.

One of the most common lessons learned from real-world SOC incidents is the critical importance of early detection. In many high-profile breaches, attackers remained undetected for weeks or even months before security teams identified malicious activity. Delayed detection often results from insufficient log visibility, ineffective correlation of security events, and an overwhelming number of false positives that distract analysts from identifying real threats. SOC teams must continuously fine-tune their Security Information and Event Management (SIEM) systems, leverage machine learning-based anomaly detection, and implement automated alert prioritization to ensure that genuine threats receive immediate attention.

A major challenge in SOC operations is the over-reliance on rule-based detection methods, which can be easily bypassed by sophisticated attackers. Many incidents have demonstrated that signature-based defenses alone are not enough to detect modern threats, especially advanced persistent threats (APTs) that use stealthy techniques to evade traditional security controls. SOCs must adopt behavioral analytics and threat intelligence-driven detection methods to identify suspicious activity that deviates from normal user behavior. User and Entity Behavior Analytics (UEBA) has proven effective in detecting insider threats, compromised credentials, and lateral movement within networks, which are often early indicators of a larger attack.

Incident response effectiveness is another critical lesson derived from real-world attacks. Many organizations have suffered greater damage due to slow response times, unclear escalation procedures, and poor coordination between security teams and business stakeholders. One case study involved a ransomware attack where the SOC detected the initial intrusion but failed to act quickly enough to contain the threat. As a result, the attackers encrypted critical business data, leading to operational disruptions and financial losses. This incident reinforced the importance of well-documented incident response playbooks, real-time collaboration tools, and the automation of containment measures using Security Orchestration, Automation, and Response (SOAR) platforms.

SOC incidents have also revealed the weaknesses in access control policies that allow attackers to escalate privileges and move laterally across the network. Many breaches occur due to excessive user permissions, lack of multi-factor authentication (MFA), and insufficient network segmentation. One notable attack involved an employee using weak credentials that were stolen through a phishing attack, giving attackers initial access to the corporate network. Once inside, they escalated privileges due to poorly configured role-based access controls (RBAC). Organizations that have experienced such incidents have implemented stricter identity and access management policies, enforcing least privilege principles and requiring MFA for all critical systems.

Phishing remains one of the most effective attack vectors, and numerous SOC incidents highlight the challenges of user awareness and email security. Despite having advanced email filtering solutions, many organizations continue to experience security breaches due to well-crafted phishing emails that bypass traditional defenses. A high-profile case involved attackers impersonating a senior executive and tricking an employee into transferring funds to an unauthorized account. Following this incident, the affected organization revised its email security policies, implemented domain-based message authentication (DMARC) protocols, and intensified phishing awareness training programs to reduce employee susceptibility to social engineering tactics.

Cloud security incidents have demonstrated the need for continuous monitoring of cloud environments. Many organizations have suffered breaches due to misconfigured cloud storage, insufficient access controls, and a lack of real-time visibility into cloud workloads. In one case, a financial services company exposed sensitive customer data because of a misconfigured Amazon S3 bucket that allowed public access. This incident highlighted the need for Cloud Security Posture Management (CSPM) solutions to automatically detect and remediate misconfigurations. Organizations that learned from similar incidents now enforce strict cloud security policies, conduct frequent audits, and integrate cloud-native security tools to monitor real-time activity.

Another significant lesson learned from real-world SOC incidents is the importance of integrating threat intelligence into security operations. Many organizations have been targeted by previously known attack techniques, but due to poor threat intelligence integration, their security teams failed to recognize the threats in time. In a major cyber espionage case, attackers reused indicators of compromise (IOCs) that were publicly available in threat intelligence reports, yet the affected organization had not implemented proactive threat hunting based on those reports. This incident reinforced the necessity of consuming, analyzing, and operationalizing threat intelligence to detect attacks before they escalate.

Collaboration between SOC teams and other business units is often tested during major security incidents. Many breaches have revealed gaps in communication between security teams, IT administrators, and executive leadership, leading to delayed decision-making and inefficient response efforts. In a notable case, an organization dealing with a distributed denial-of-service (DDoS) attack struggled to coordinate between SOC analysts and IT infrastructure teams, resulting in prolonged downtime. This incident emphasized the importance of cross-functional incident response exercises, clear communication protocols, and the use of real-time collaboration platforms to streamline decision-making during crises.

The role of post-incident analysis is another critical takeaway from real-world breaches. Many organizations fail to conduct thorough post-mortem reviews, leading to repeated security failures. In one case, an organization was hit by two nearly identical ransomware attacks within six months because the first incident was not properly analyzed, and security gaps remained unaddressed. Organizations that have experienced repeated security failures now prioritize lessons-learned reviews, conduct root cause analyses, and implement continuous improvement processes to prevent future incidents.

Regulatory compliance and legal implications often become major concerns following significant security incidents. Organizations that fail to comply with data protection regulations face fines, legal action, and reputational damage. In one case, a healthcare provider suffered a data breach and was later fined under HIPAA regulations for failing to implement adequate security controls. This incident served as a reminder that compliance should not be viewed as a checkbox exercise but rather as an integral part of cybersecurity governance. SOCs that have learned from similar cases now work closely with compliance officers to ensure that security policies align with regulatory requirements.

Real-world SOC incidents provide a wealth of knowledge that helps organizations refine their cybersecurity strategies, enhance detection and response capabilities, and improve overall security resilience. By analyzing past breaches, organizations can identify weaknesses in security tools, improve incident response playbooks, and strengthen user awareness programs. Continuous learning from real incidents ensures that SOCs evolve to counter emerging threats, reducing the risk of future breaches and minimizing the impact of cyberattacks.

SOC Staffing Challenges and Workforce Development

Staffing a Security Operations Center (SOC) presents significant challenges for organizations due to the growing demand for cybersecurity professionals, the complexity of modern threats, and the need for continuous skill development. SOC teams are responsible for monitoring, detecting, and responding to cyber threats in real time, requiring highly skilled analysts, threat hunters, incident responders, and security engineers. However, many organizations struggle to recruit and retain qualified personnel, leading to staff shortages, burnout, and operational inefficiencies. Workforce development is a crucial component of SOC success, ensuring that security teams have the necessary expertise, training, and career growth opportunities to meet the evolving demands of cybersecurity.

One of the primary challenges in SOC staffing is the global cybersecurity talent shortage. The increasing number of cyber threats has created a high demand for skilled security professionals, yet there are not enough qualified candidates to fill open positions. Organizations often compete for the same limited pool of talent, making it difficult to hire experienced SOC analysts. This talent gap forces many SOCs to rely on junior personnel who require extensive training before they can handle complex security incidents. The lack of skilled professionals also results in an overburdened workforce, where analysts are expected to manage an overwhelming number of alerts and security events with limited resources.

SOC burnout is a major concern due to the high-stress nature of the job. Security analysts often work in a fast-paced environment where they must respond to continuous threats, investigate security incidents, and analyze large volumes of security logs. The constant pressure to detect and mitigate threats can lead to fatigue, reduced job satisfaction, and high turnover rates. Many SOC analysts experience alert fatigue, where they must sift through thousands of alerts, many of which are false positives, making it difficult to identify real threats. Organizations that fail to address analyst burnout risk losing valuable talent and reducing the effectiveness of their SOC operations.

To mitigate staffing challenges, organizations must invest in workforce development programs that enhance the skills of SOC personnel and provide clear career progression paths. Training and certification programs help bridge the skills gap by equipping analysts with the knowledge needed to handle advanced security threats. Industry-recognized certifications, such as Certified Information Systems Security Professional (CISSP), Certified Ethical Hacker (CEH), and GIAC Security Essentials (GSEC), provide a structured learning path for SOC analysts to expand their expertise. Many organizations also offer in-house training programs, mentorship opportunities, and hands-on labs to help analysts gain practical experience in threat detection and incident response.

Automation and artificial intelligence (AI) can help alleviate SOC staffing shortages by reducing the manual workload on security analysts. Security Orchestration, Automation, and Response (SOAR) platforms streamline incident response processes by automating routine tasks, such as alert triage, threat intelligence enrichment, and incident reporting. AI-powered security analytics improve threat detection by identifying patterns in security data, reducing false positives, and allowing analysts to focus on high-priority incidents. By integrating automation into SOC workflows, organizations can maximize the efficiency of their existing workforce and reduce the reliance on large security teams.

Outsourcing SOC functions to Managed Security Service Providers (MSSPs) is another strategy for addressing staffing challenges. MSSPs provide organizations with access to experienced security professionals, 24/7 monitoring capabilities, and specialized threat intelligence services. While outsourcing can help reduce the burden on in-house teams, organizations must ensure that MSSP contracts include clear service level agreements (SLAs), incident response coordination plans, and data protection measures. A hybrid approach, where internal SOC teams handle critical security operations while MSSPs manage routine monitoring tasks, allows organizations to balance cost-effectiveness with operational efficiency.

Cross-training and internal talent development are effective ways to build a strong SOC workforce. Organizations can identify employees with IT, networking, or software development backgrounds who are interested in transitioning into cybersecurity roles. By providing structured training programs, hands-on labs, and job rotation opportunities, organizations can develop cybersecurity talent from within. Cross-training IT personnel in security operations helps create a more resilient workforce and reduces dependency on external hiring. Many successful SOCs have adopted apprenticeship programs that allow junior analysts to work alongside experienced security professionals and gain real-world experience in threat detection and response.

Diversity and inclusion initiatives play an important role in addressing SOC staffing challenges. The cybersecurity industry has historically struggled with workforce diversity, limiting the pool of available talent. Encouraging diversity in hiring practices, supporting women and underrepresented groups in cybersecurity careers, and promoting inclusive workplace cultures can help organizations attract and retain a broader range of skilled professionals. Partnering with universities, technical training programs, and cybersecurity boot camps focused on diversity can help organizations build a more inclusive SOC workforce.

Retaining SOC personnel requires organizations to create a positive work environment that fosters career growth, professional development, and work-life balance. Many SOC analysts leave their roles due to lack of advancement opportunities or excessive workloads. Providing career progression paths, leadership development programs, and specialized training tracks for incident responders, threat hunters, and security engineers can help retain top talent. Organizations that invest in employee well-being, offer competitive salaries, and implement flexible work arrangements are more likely to reduce turnover and build a sustainable SOC team.

Gamification and hands-on training methods can improve SOC workforce engagement and skill development. Many organizations have adopted cybersecurity capture-the-flag (CTF) competitions, red team/blue team exercises, and threat hunting challenges to help analysts refine their skills in a dynamic environment. Interactive training platforms that simulate real-world attack scenarios provide analysts with valuable experience in identifying, investigating, and mitigating threats. Continuous learning opportunities keep SOC teams engaged and motivated while ensuring that they stay ahead of evolving cyber threats.

Workforce development should also include collaboration with academia and cybersecurity education programs. Partnering with universities, technical schools, and online training providers allows organizations to create internship programs, research initiatives, and mentorship opportunities for aspiring cybersecurity professionals. Sponsoring cybersecurity competitions, offering scholarships, and participating in industry conferences help organizations connect with emerging talent and encourage students to pursue careers in SOC operations. Organizations that engage with the academic community contribute to the development of the next generation of cybersecurity professionals.

Addressing SOC staffing challenges requires a multifaceted approach that includes workforce development, automation, cross-training, outsourcing, diversity initiatives, and employee retention strategies. Organizations that proactively invest in building a skilled and resilient security workforce can overcome the talent shortage, improve SOC efficiency, and enhance their ability to detect and respond to cyber threats. By fostering a culture of continuous learning, professional growth, and innovation, SOCs can strengthen their cybersecurity posture and effectively manage the ever-evolving threat landscape.

Measuring and Improving SOC Effectiveness

A Security Operations Center (SOC) is a critical component of an organization's cybersecurity defense, responsible for monitoring, detecting, and responding to cyber threats in real time. However, simply having a SOC in place does not guarantee security effectiveness. To ensure that a SOC operates efficiently and provides value to the organization, it is essential to measure its effectiveness through key performance indicators (KPIs), continuous monitoring, and regular assessments. By implementing structured improvement strategies,

SOC teams can enhance their ability to detect threats, reduce response times, and strengthen overall security posture.

Measuring SOC effectiveness begins with defining clear objectives that align with the organization's cybersecurity goals. A SOC must balance three core functions: proactive threat detection, rapid incident response, and continuous security improvement. Key performance indicators help SOC teams evaluate how well these functions are being executed and identify areas that require enhancement. Organizations must establish performance benchmarks based on industry standards, regulatory requirements, and evolving threat landscapes to ensure that their SOC remains aligned with best practices.

One of the most critical metrics for evaluating SOC effectiveness is Mean Time to Detect (MTTD), which measures the average time it takes for the SOC to identify a security threat. A low MTTD indicates that the SOC has strong monitoring capabilities and can quickly recognize potential threats before they escalate into major incidents. If MTTD is high, it may signal gaps in threat intelligence integration, insufficient log correlation, or inadequate security analytics. Improving MTTD requires optimizing Security Information and Event Management (SIEM) configurations, refining detection rules, and leveraging advanced behavioral analytics to enhance anomaly detection.

Mean Time to Respond (MTTR) is another crucial metric that evaluates the SOC's ability to contain and mitigate security threats after detection. A high MTTR suggests that the SOC is struggling with inefficient response workflows, lack of automation, or delays in incident escalation. Reducing MTTR involves streamlining incident response procedures, implementing playbooks for common attack scenarios, and integrating Security Orchestration, Automation, and Response (SOAR) platforms to automate containment actions. By improving response efficiency, SOC teams can minimize the impact of cyber threats and reduce potential downtime.

False positive rates play a significant role in determining SOC efficiency. High false positive rates indicate that analysts are spending excessive time investigating benign security alerts, leading to alert fatigue and resource wastage. If too many false positives occur, legitimate threats may be overlooked or delayed in detection. SOC teams must continuously refine detection mechanisms, eliminate redundant security rules, and incorporate machine learning models that improve alert accuracy. Regularly tuning SIEM correlation rules and leveraging threat intelligence feeds help enhance alert fidelity, ensuring that analysts focus on real threats rather than noise.

Threat detection coverage is another important factor in assessing SOC performance. Organizations must evaluate whether their SOC has visibility across all critical assets, including endpoints, network traffic, cloud environments, and third-party integrations. Gaps in coverage can leave the organization vulnerable to undetected threats. SOC teams should conduct regular security audits, penetration tests, and red team exercises to validate detection capabilities. Expanding log sources, improving endpoint visibility with Endpoint Detection and Response (EDR) solutions, and integrating cloud-native security tools enhance SOC coverage and ensure that no blind spots exist.

Incident escalation efficiency is a key determinant of SOC effectiveness. Security teams must have well-defined escalation procedures to ensure that critical incidents are addressed by the appropriate personnel without unnecessary delays. Delays in escalation can lead to prolonged attacker dwell time and increased business impact. SOCs must establish clear severity classifications for incidents, automate alert prioritization, and implement structured handoff processes between Tier 1, Tier 2, and Tier 3 analysts. Training analysts on escalation best practices and conducting regular incident response drills improve decision-making under pressure.

Post-incident analysis and continuous improvement are essential for refining SOC operations. Every security incident provides valuable lessons that can enhance future detection and response capabilities. Conducting root cause analyses, documenting lessons learned, and updating security policies based on real-world incidents ensure that SOC teams evolve with emerging threats. Incident response post-mortems help identify weaknesses in detection tools, gaps in response workflows, and opportunities for process optimization. SOCs that prioritize post-incident reviews continuously improve their resilience against cyber threats.

Threat hunting is an advanced security practice that complements SOC monitoring by proactively searching for hidden threats that may evade traditional detection mechanisms. Effective threat hunting programs improve SOC effectiveness by identifying previously undetected attacks, uncovering persistent threats, and strengthening overall security intelligence. SOCs should establish dedicated threat hunting teams, leverage historical security data for anomaly detection, and integrate threat intelligence-driven hunting techniques. Encouraging a proactive security mindset among analysts fosters a culture of continuous threat discovery and mitigation.

Security awareness training within the SOC enhances effectiveness by ensuring that analysts remain updated on the latest attack techniques, security tools, and best practices. Cyber threats evolve rapidly, requiring SOC teams to continuously develop their skills through training programs, industry certifications, and participation in cybersecurity exercises. Encouraging analysts to obtain certifications such as Certified Information Systems Security Professional (CISSP), GIAC Certified Incident Handler (GCIH), and Offensive Security Certified Professional (OSCP) strengthens their expertise and enhances SOC performance.

Collaboration and information sharing play a vital role in SOC improvement. Organizations should actively participate in threat intelligence-sharing communities, engage with industry groups, and collaborate with government cybersecurity agencies to stay ahead of emerging threats. By exchanging threat intelligence, SOC teams gain insights into attack trends, learn from incidents affecting other organizations, and enhance their ability to detect sophisticated adversaries. Threat intelligence platforms (TIPs) facilitate automated intelligence sharing, enabling SOC teams to integrate external threat data into their security operations seamlessly.

Regular SOC maturity assessments help organizations benchmark their security operations against industry best practices. Maturity models such as the MITRE ATT&CK framework, NIST Cybersecurity Framework, and the Capability Maturity Model Integration (CMMI) provide structured approaches for evaluating SOC effectiveness. These assessments help identify strengths, weaknesses, and areas requiring investment to enhance SOC capabilities. Organizations should conduct periodic gap analyses, implement improvement roadmaps, and allocate resources to strengthen identified weaknesses.

Leadership engagement and executive buy-in are critical for sustaining SOC improvements. SOC teams must effectively communicate their value to organizational leadership by demonstrating tangible security improvements, cost savings, and risk reduction benefits. Regular executive briefings, security performance reports, and real-world incident case studies help align SOC initiatives with business priorities. Organizations that prioritize cybersecurity at the leadership level ensure that SOC teams receive the necessary funding, resources, and strategic direction to enhance effectiveness.

An effective SOC is one that continuously evolves, adapts to emerging threats, and refines its operations based on measurable performance indicators. By focusing on key metrics such as MTTD, MTTR, false positive rates, and threat detection coverage, organizations can assess their SOC's strengths and weaknesses. Implementing structured improvement strategies, leveraging automation, enhancing analyst training, and fostering a culture of continuous learning contribute to the long-term success of SOC operations. Cybersecurity is an ongoing battle, and organizations that prioritize SOC effectiveness are better equipped to defend against the ever-evolving threat landscape.

Conducting SOC Tabletop Exercises and Drills

Tabletop exercises and drills are essential components of an effective Security Operations Center (SOC), providing security teams with hands-on experience in responding to cyber threats. These exercises simulate real-world attack scenarios, allowing SOC analysts, incident responders, and IT teams to practice their detection, containment, and mitigation strategies in a controlled environment. By conducting structured tabletop exercises and technical drills, organizations can identify weaknesses in their security posture, refine incident response procedures, and improve collaboration among key stakeholders. Regularly testing response capabilities ensures that SOC teams are prepared to handle actual security incidents with efficiency and confidence.

Tabletop exercises focus on decision-making and coordination rather than technical execution. These exercises involve SOC teams, IT administrators, executive leadership, legal representatives, and other relevant stakeholders who play a role in cybersecurity incident response. A facilitator presents a hypothetical security incident, guiding participants through various stages of detection, containment, investigation, and resolution. Participants discuss how they would respond to the incident, document their decisions, and evaluate the effectiveness of their communication and coordination strategies. Tabletop exercises help organizations identify gaps in incident response planning, improve cross-functional collaboration, and refine escalation procedures.

Technical drills, on the other hand, are hands-on exercises designed to test the technical skills of SOC analysts and incident responders. These drills involve real-time simulations of cyberattacks, such as phishing campaigns, ransomware infections, distributed denial-of-service (DDoS) attacks, and insider threats. Unlike tabletop exercises, which focus on high-level strategy, technical drills require SOC teams to actively analyze security alerts, investigate anomalies, and deploy containment measures. Conducting technical drills ensures that analysts can effectively utilize security tools, interpret threat intelligence, and execute response actions under realistic conditions.

The first step in conducting a successful tabletop exercise is defining the objectives and scope of the simulation. Organizations must determine what aspects of incident response they want to evaluate, whether it be threat detection, communication protocols, regulatory compliance, or forensic investigation capabilities. The scope should align with the organization's security priorities, risk profile, and regulatory obligations. Some exercises may focus on a specific attack vector, such as business email compromise (BEC), while others may test the organization's ability to handle large-scale data breaches. Clearly defining objectives ensures that the exercise delivers actionable insights that lead to meaningful improvements.

Scenario development is a critical component of both tabletop exercises and technical drills. Scenarios should be based on realistic threats that the organization is likely to encounter, incorporating elements from recent cyber incidents, industry threat intelligence, and adversary tactics from frameworks such as MITRE ATT&CK. The complexity of the scenario should match the experience level of the participants, ensuring that the exercise is challenging but achievable. A well-designed scenario includes multiple phases of an attack, allowing SOC teams to test their ability to detect initial compromise, track adversary movement, and mitigate the threat before significant damage occurs.

During a tabletop exercise, the facilitator presents the scenario in stages, prompting participants to discuss their actions at each phase of the incident. Questions such as "How would your team detect this attack?" or "What steps would you take to contain the breach?" help guide the discussion. Participants must explain their reasoning, document their decisions, and consider the potential consequences of their actions. The exercise should encourage critical thinking, collaboration, and adherence to predefined incident response playbooks. The facilitator may introduce unexpected developments, such as data exfiltration or regulatory reporting requirements, to test the team's adaptability under pressure.

Technical drills require a more hands-on approach, often utilizing red team simulations, adversary emulation platforms, or dedicated cyber ranges. SOC analysts engage with simulated attack data, analyze security logs, and respond to active threats using security tools such as Security Information and Event Management (SIEM) platforms, Endpoint Detection and Response (EDR) solutions, and network forensics tools. These drills help SOC teams improve their investigative techniques, enhance threat-hunting capabilities, and validate the effectiveness of automated detection mechanisms. Organizations can use breach and attack simulation (BAS) tools to automate these exercises and continuously assess security defenses.

One of the key benefits of tabletop exercises and technical drills is improving communication and coordination between different teams involved in incident response. Many security incidents require collaboration between SOC analysts, IT administrators, legal teams, human resources, and executive leadership. Tabletop exercises help clarify roles and responsibilities, ensuring that each team understands its function in mitigating security incidents. Regular participation in these exercises builds confidence, reduces confusion during real incidents, and enhances the organization's overall response efficiency.

Regulatory compliance is another important aspect of SOC exercises. Many data protection regulations, such as the General Data Protection Regulation (GDPR), the Health Insurance Portability and Accountability Act (HIPAA), and the Payment Card Industry Data Security Standard (PCI DSS), require organizations to demonstrate their ability to respond to security incidents effectively. Tabletop exercises provide an opportunity to test compliance with regulatory reporting requirements, ensuring that organizations are prepared to notify customers, regulators, and stakeholders in the event of a data breach. Exercises also help assess whether data retention, access control, and forensic investigation processes align with legal obligations.

Post-exercise analysis is essential for maximizing the value of tabletop exercises and technical drills. After each exercise, SOC teams should conduct a structured debriefing to review their performance, document key takeaways, and identify areas for improvement. Facilitators should provide feedback on decision-making, response times, and coordination effectiveness. SOC teams should update incident response playbooks, refine security policies, and implement new detection rules based on lessons learned. Continuous refinement of response procedures ensures that the organization evolves its defenses against emerging cyber threats.

Organizations should conduct tabletop exercises and technical drills on a regular basis to maintain SOC readiness. Cyber threats constantly evolve, requiring security teams to adapt their detection and response strategies accordingly. Scheduling quarterly or semi-annual exercises ensures that SOC personnel remain familiar with incident response protocols, while periodic technical drills reinforce practical skills. Organizations can also introduce unannounced exercises, known as "live fire drills," to test how well teams react to unexpected security incidents in real time.

Collaboration with external security partners enhances the effectiveness of SOC exercises. Many organizations engage third-party cybersecurity firms to conduct red team assessments, provide adversary simulations, or facilitate training exercises. Partnering with industry threat intelligence groups, government agencies, and information-sharing communities can also provide valuable insights into emerging attack trends and best practices for incident response. Sharing lessons learned from SOC exercises with peer organizations helps improve collective defense efforts against cyber threats.

Conducting tabletop exercises and technical drills is a proactive approach to strengthening SOC capabilities, improving threat detection and response, and ensuring organizational resilience against cyberattacks. By regularly testing security protocols, enhancing cross-team collaboration, and refining incident response strategies, SOC teams can maintain operational readiness and minimize the impact of security incidents. The ability to effectively manage cyber threats depends not only on security technology but also on the preparedness and coordination of the people responsible for defending the organization.

The Future of SOCs: Trends and Innovations

Security Operations Centers (SOCs) are at the forefront of defending organizations against increasingly sophisticated cyber threats. As cyberattacks grow in complexity, SOCs must continuously evolve to keep pace with adversaries, emerging technologies, and the ever-expanding attack surface. The future of SOCs will be shaped by advancements in artificial intelligence, automation, cloud security, extended detection and response (XDR), zero trust architecture, and new workforce development strategies. These innovations will enable SOCs to become more efficient, adaptive, and proactive in detecting and mitigating threats in real time.

One of the most significant trends influencing the future of SOCs is the widespread adoption of artificial intelligence (AI) and machine learning (ML). Traditional SOCs rely heavily on human analysts to investigate security alerts, correlate data, and identify threats. However, the sheer volume of security events has outpaced the capacity of manual analysis. AI-driven security analytics are transforming SOC operations by automating threat detection, reducing false positives, and identifying anomalies that may indicate malicious activity. Machine learning models continuously improve over time by analyzing vast amounts of security data, enabling SOCs to detect previously unknown attack patterns and emerging threats with greater accuracy.

Automation is another critical innovation that will redefine SOC efficiency. Security Orchestration, Automation, and Response (SOAR) platforms are revolutionizing the way security teams handle incidents by automating repetitive tasks such as alert triage, threat intelligence enrichment, and incident containment. Automated workflows enable SOC analysts to focus on more complex investigations rather than spending time on routine administrative tasks. As SOAR platforms become more advanced, they will integrate seamlessly with SIEM (Security Information and Event Management), Endpoint Detection and Response (EDR), and other security tools to provide a fully automated incident response framework. The use of robotic process automation (RPA) in SOCs is also expected to streamline security operations by handling high-volume tasks such as log analysis and forensic data collection.

Cloud security is another area where SOCs must adapt rapidly. As organizations migrate workloads, applications, and data to cloud environments, traditional perimeter-based security models become obsolete. The shift to cloud-native security solutions, including Cloud Security Posture Management (CSPM) and Cloud Workload Protection Platforms (CWPP), is transforming how SOCs monitor cloud environments for threats. SOCs of the future will need to integrate cloud security monitoring tools that provide real-time visibility into multi-cloud environments, detect misconfigurations, and enforce compliance policies across hybrid infrastructures. Cloud-native extended detection and response (XDR) solutions will enhance SOC capabilities by unifying security telemetry from endpoints, networks, and cloud workloads into a single detection and response framework.

Extended Detection and Response (XDR) is emerging as a game-changing innovation for SOCs by breaking down silos between different security tools. Unlike traditional SIEMs that primarily aggregate log data, XDR platforms provide deeper security analytics, cross-layer correlation, and automated response capabilities. XDR integrates data from endpoints, networks, identity systems, and cloud environments to create a unified security ecosystem. By leveraging AI-driven analytics, XDR improves threat detection accuracy and speeds up investigation processes. Future SOCs will likely adopt XDR as a core technology, replacing fragmented security solutions with a more cohesive and efficient approach to threat detection and response.

The adoption of zero trust security models will also influence the evolution of SOCs. Zero trust is based on the principle of "never trust, always verify," meaning that every access request is continuously validated, regardless of whether it originates inside or outside the network perimeter. Traditional SOCs often focus on external threat detection, but as insider threats and supply chain attacks increase, zero trust will become an essential component of SOC strategies. Future SOCs will leverage identity-based security, micro-segmentation, and continuous authentication to enforce zero trust policies. This approach will enable SOC teams to detect and prevent lateral movement within networks, reducing the impact of potential breaches.

Threat intelligence will play an even greater role in shaping the future of SOC operations. As cyber threats become more sophisticated, SOCs will need to rely on real-time threat intelligence feeds, predictive analytics, and advanced threat hunting techniques to stay ahead of attackers. AI-driven threat intelligence platforms will provide automated correlation of global threat data, enabling SOC analysts to anticipate cyber threats before they materialize. Threat intelligence-sharing communities and industry collaboration will continue to grow, allowing SOCs to gain deeper insights into adversary tactics, techniques, and procedures (TTPs). Future SOCs will not only react to known threats but will proactively hunt for emerging threats using adversary emulation and proactive cyber defense strategies.

The evolution of SOC staffing and workforce development will be another key trend shaping the future of security operations. The cybersecurity skills gap remains a significant challenge, with organizations struggling to find and retain skilled SOC analysts. To address this issue, SOCs will increasingly rely on AI-driven virtual analysts, gamified training programs, and cybersecurity apprenticeships to develop new talent. Cyber range environments and simulated attack scenarios will be used to train SOC analysts in real-world threat detection and incident response. Organizations will also adopt hybrid workforce models, leveraging a combination of in-house SOC personnel, managed security service providers (MSSPs), and remote security analysts to provide 24/7 threat monitoring.

Decentralized SOC models are also emerging as a response to the growing complexity of global cybersecurity threats. Traditional SOCs operate from centralized locations, but future SOCs may adopt decentralized architectures where security monitoring is distributed across multiple regional or cloud-based SOCs. This approach improves scalability, enhances resilience against localized disruptions, and enables security teams to operate more effectively in hybrid work environments. Organizations will adopt federated SOC models, where multiple SOCs collaborate across geographic regions while sharing a unified security strategy and common threat intelligence.

The convergence of IT and operational technology (OT) security will further influence SOC transformation. As cyber-physical systems, industrial control systems (ICS), and Internet of Things (IoT) devices become more interconnected, SOCs must expand their monitoring capabilities to include non-traditional IT environments. Future SOCs will integrate OT security tools, industrial threat intelligence platforms, and AI-driven anomaly detection systems to protect critical infrastructure from cyber threats. The integration of IT and OT security within SOCs will require specialized training for analysts, ensuring that security teams understand both traditional network threats and industrial cyber risks.

Regulatory and compliance frameworks will continue to shape SOC strategies, requiring organizations to enhance their security monitoring and reporting capabilities. Governments and regulatory bodies are implementing stricter cybersecurity laws, requiring organizations to demonstrate continuous security monitoring, incident response readiness, and compliance with data protection regulations. Future SOCs will need to integrate compliance automation tools, real-time audit tracking, and automated reporting systems to meet regulatory requirements efficiently.

As cyber threats evolve, SOCs must embrace innovation, automation, and adaptive security models to stay ahead of adversaries. The integration of AI, SOAR, XDR, cloud-native security, and zero trust frameworks will define the next generation of SOC operations. By investing in cutting-edge security technologies, workforce development, and proactive threat intelligence strategies, organizations will build SOCs that are more efficient, resilient, and capable of defending against the cyber threats of the future. The continued evolution of SOCs will not only enhance security operations but will also redefine the way organizations approach cybersecurity as a whole.

Scaling and Expanding a SOC for Growth

As organizations grow, their Security Operations Centers (SOCs) must evolve to handle increasing security demands, new technologies, and expanding attack surfaces. Scaling a SOC requires a strategic approach that balances technological advancements, process optimizations, workforce development, and resource allocation. A SOC that fails to scale effectively may struggle with alert fatigue, delayed threat detection, and operational inefficiencies, leaving the organization vulnerable to cyber threats. Expansion must be carefully planned to ensure that SOC operations remain agile, efficient, and capable of responding to evolving cybersecurity challenges.

One of the first considerations when scaling a SOC is the need for increased security visibility across an expanding IT infrastructure. As organizations grow, they introduce new endpoints, cloud environments, third-party integrations, and operational technology (OT) systems, all of which must be monitored for security threats. Scaling a SOC requires implementing security tools that can handle larger data volumes without overwhelming analysts. Security Information and Event Management (SIEM) solutions must be capable of ingesting and correlating logs from diverse sources while maintaining high performance. Upgrading SIEM platforms or transitioning to extended detection and response (XDR) solutions can improve threat visibility and reduce data silos, ensuring that security teams can effectively monitor expanding environments.

Automation plays a crucial role in scaling SOC operations efficiently. As security teams face increasing alert volumes, manual incident response processes become unsustainable. Security Orchestration, Automation, and Response (SOAR) platforms enable SOCs to automate repetitive tasks such as threat enrichment, alert triage, and incident containment. By leveraging automation, SOCs can reduce response times, minimize human error, and allow analysts to focus on high-priority threats. Automated playbooks ensure consistency in response actions, enabling SOC teams to scale their operations without a proportional increase in staffing requirements.

Expanding a SOC also requires optimizing workflows and incident response procedures. As the number of security incidents grows, SOC teams must refine their escalation protocols to prevent bottlenecks and delays. Implementing a tiered response structure, where Tier 1 analysts handle initial triage, Tier 2 analysts conduct deeper investigations, and Tier 3 specialists manage advanced threat hunting, ensures that security events are processed efficiently. Regular reviews of incident response playbooks, incorporating lessons learned from past incidents, help streamline operations and improve SOC agility.

Workforce expansion is another critical factor in SOC scalability. As organizations grow, SOC teams must be adequately staffed to manage increasing security demands. Hiring skilled security analysts can be challenging due to the cybersecurity skills gap, making workforce development programs essential. Organizations should invest in training programs, mentorship initiatives, and certification pathways to upskill existing IT professionals into security roles. Establishing an apprenticeship model, where junior analysts work alongside experienced threat hunters and incident responders, accelerates skill development and ensures that the SOC has a steady pipeline of trained personnel.

Hybrid SOC models provide a scalable approach to expanding security operations while optimizing resource utilization. Organizations may choose to maintain an in-house SOC for core security functions while outsourcing certain aspects of security monitoring to Managed Security Service Providers (MSSPs) or Managed Detection and Response (MDR) providers. This approach allows organizations to scale their security capabilities without the overhead of hiring and training additional personnel. MSSPs provide 24/7 threat monitoring, while internal SOC teams focus on strategic security initiatives, incident response, and compliance management.

Cloud security expansion is a major consideration for scaling SOCs, as organizations increasingly migrate workloads to public, private, and hybrid cloud environments. Traditional SOCs designed for on-premises infrastructure may struggle to monitor cloud-native assets effectively. Implementing Cloud Security Posture Management (CSPM) and Cloud Workload Protection Platforms (CWPP) helps SOC teams gain visibility into cloud misconfigurations, unauthorized access attempts, and data exfiltration risks. Security monitoring must extend beyond on-premises networks to encompass multi-cloud environments, Software-as-a-Service (SaaS) applications, and containerized workloads.

As organizations expand internationally or across multiple locations, SOCs must adapt to decentralized security operations. A single centralized SOC may not be sufficient to provide real-time threat detection across geographically dispersed networks. Organizations can implement a follow-the-sun SOC model, where security teams across different time zones provide continuous threat monitoring and incident response. Distributed SOC architectures enable organizations to allocate security responsibilities based on regional expertise, regulatory requirements, and language considerations. Ensuring seamless communication and collaboration between global SOC teams is essential for maintaining consistent security operations.

Threat intelligence integration is another key factor in SOC expansion. As organizations grow, they become more attractive targets for advanced persistent threats (APTs), nation-state actors, and cybercriminal organizations. Scaling a SOC requires access to real-time threat intelligence feeds, adversary tactics, techniques, and procedures (TTPs), and industry threat-sharing communities. Threat intelligence platforms (TIPs) provide automated correlation of external threat data with internal security events, helping SOC analysts identify and prioritize emerging threats. By leveraging intelligence-driven security operations, organizations can proactively defend against evolving cyber risks.

Security compliance and regulatory requirements also play a significant role in SOC expansion. As organizations enter new markets, acquire subsidiaries, or handle sensitive data, they must comply with industry regulations such as the General Data Protection Regulation (GDPR), the Health Insurance Portability and Accountability Act (HIPAA), and the Payment Card Industry Data Security Standard (PCI DSS). Scaling a SOC requires implementing compliance automation tools that streamline audit reporting, enforce data protection policies, and ensure continuous adherence to regulatory requirements. Proactively aligning security operations with compliance frameworks prevents legal and financial risks associated with non-compliance.

Incident response scalability is another important consideration when expanding SOC capabilities. Large-scale incidents, such as ransomware outbreaks or supply chain attacks, require rapid coordination between multiple teams, including IT, legal, public relations, and executive leadership. Organizations should develop crisis management frameworks that outline roles, responsibilities, and escalation procedures for high-impact security incidents. Conducting regular tabletop exercises, red team assessments, and full-scale incident response simulations helps SOC teams prepare for large-scale threats and improve cross-functional coordination.

SOCs must also consider security tool integration and interoperability when scaling their operations. A fragmented security stack with disconnected tools can lead to inefficiencies, visibility gaps, and delayed threat detection. Organizations should prioritize security solutions that support open APIs, standardized data exchange formats, and seamless integrations with existing infrastructure. Unified security architectures that consolidate threat detection, response, and analytics enhance SOC efficiency and reduce operational complexity.

Performance metrics and key performance indicators (KPIs) play a crucial role in assessing SOC scalability. Organizations should track metrics such as Mean Time to Detect (MTTD), Mean Time to Respond (MTTR), false positive rates, and threat coverage to evaluate SOC effectiveness. As SOCs scale, they must continuously refine their detection algorithms, optimize response workflows, and invest in security automation to maintain high efficiency. Regular SOC maturity assessments help organizations benchmark their security operations against industry best practices and identify areas for further improvement.

Scaling and expanding a SOC requires a strategic balance of technology, automation, workforce development, and operational optimization. Organizations must continuously adapt their security operations to meet evolving cyber threats, regulatory requirements, and business growth demands. By leveraging cloud security solutions, automation, threat intelligence, and hybrid SOC models, organizations can build scalable and resilient security operations that provide robust protection against advanced cyber threats. An effectively scaled SOC not only enhances threat detection and response but also ensures long-term security sustainability as organizations continue to grow.

Common Pitfalls When Building a SOC and How to Avoid Them

Building a Security Operations Center (SOC) is a complex undertaking that requires careful planning, the right mix of technology, skilled personnel, and well-defined processes. Organizations often invest significant resources in setting up a SOC, only to encounter operational inefficiencies, misaligned objectives, and security gaps that hinder their ability to detect and respond to cyber threats effectively. Identifying and understanding common pitfalls in SOC development can help organizations avoid costly mistakes and create a high-functioning security operation that delivers real value.

One of the most common pitfalls when building a SOC is a lack of clearly defined objectives. Many organizations establish a SOC without first determining its purpose, scope, and alignment with business goals. Without clear objectives, SOC teams may struggle to prioritize threats, allocate resources effectively, or measure success. Organizations must define whether their SOC will focus on real-time threat monitoring, regulatory compliance, incident response, or advanced threat hunting. Aligning the SOC's objectives with the organization's risk management strategy ensures that security operations are relevant, effective, and capable of supporting broader business needs.

An overreliance on technology without a corresponding investment in people and processes is another major challenge. Many organizations assume that purchasing a Security Information and Event Management (SIEM) system, Endpoint Detection and Response (EDR) tools, or Security Orchestration, Automation, and Response (SOAR) platforms will automatically enhance security operations. While these technologies are essential, they must be properly configured, monitored, and managed by skilled analysts. SOC teams need continuous training to effectively interpret security alerts, investigate incidents, and fine-tune detection rules. A technology-first approach without adequate workforce investment often leads to tool misconfigurations, alert fatigue, and overlooked security threats.

Alert fatigue is a critical issue that can overwhelm SOC analysts and lead to missed threats. A poorly configured SOC may generate thousands of false positives daily, making it difficult for analysts to distinguish real threats from noise. This problem arises when detection rules are too broad, SIEM filters are not optimized, or threat intelligence feeds are not properly tuned. To address alert fatigue, organizations must refine detection logic, implement behavioral analytics, and leverage machine learning to reduce false positives. Prioritizing alerts based on risk severity and automating low-priority investigations can help analysts focus on genuine security incidents.

Failure to establish well-defined incident response procedures can severely impact a SOC's ability to handle threats efficiently. Some organizations build a SOC without implementing structured response playbooks, leading to inconsistent threat handling, confusion during incidents, and delayed mitigation efforts. Incident response frameworks should outline step-by-step procedures for different attack scenarios, define escalation protocols, and ensure that all stakeholders understand their roles and responsibilities. Regular incident response drills, tabletop exercises, and live-fire simulations help reinforce response procedures and prepare SOC teams for real-world attacks.

A lack of integration between security tools can create visibility gaps and hinder threat detection efforts. Many organizations deploy multiple security solutions, such as firewalls, SIEMs, endpoint security tools, and network detection systems, without ensuring seamless interoperability. Disconnected security tools result in fragmented data, delayed investigations, and difficulty correlating security events across different environments. To avoid this issue, organizations should prioritize solutions that support open APIs, centralized dashboards, and automated data correlation. A unified SOC platform that aggregates threat intelligence, log data, and response workflows enhances visibility and improves detection accuracy.

Underestimating the importance of threat intelligence is another pitfall that weakens SOC effectiveness. Some organizations focus exclusively on internal security monitoring and fail to leverage external threat intelligence sources to anticipate attacks. Threat intelligence provides valuable insights into emerging threats, adversary tactics, and indicators of compromise (IOCs) that can improve proactive threat detection. Organizations should integrate real-time threat intelligence feeds into their SOC operations, participate in industry threat-sharing communities, and conduct regular threat-hunting exercises based on intelligence data. Failure to incorporate threat intelligence leads to a reactive SOC rather than a proactive one.

SOC staffing challenges often undermine security operations. Many organizations struggle to recruit and retain skilled SOC analysts due to the global cybersecurity skills shortage. High turnover rates, burnout, and lack of career progression can lead to operational inefficiencies and knowledge gaps. Organizations must implement structured workforce development programs, offer competitive compensation, and provide career growth opportunities to retain skilled personnel. Cross-training IT staff in cybersecurity roles and leveraging managed security service providers (MSSPs) for supplemental support can help address staffing limitations. Investing in automation tools to handle repetitive tasks also reduces the workload on analysts, improving job satisfaction and retention.

Ignoring cloud security when building a SOC is a growing concern as organizations migrate workloads to cloud environments. Traditional SOCs designed for on-premises infrastructure often lack visibility into cloud applications, containers, and serverless architectures. Cloud misconfigurations, unauthorized access, and API vulnerabilities introduce new attack vectors that must be monitored. Organizations must integrate cloud-native security tools, such as Cloud Security Posture Management (CSPM) and Cloud Workload Protection Platforms (CWPP), into their SOC workflows. Continuous cloud security monitoring ensures that organizations can detect and respond to threats in hybrid and multi-cloud environments.

Another mistake organizations make is failing to conduct regular SOC maturity assessments. Once a SOC is operational, it must continuously evolve to keep pace with emerging threats, regulatory changes, and organizational growth. Many SOCs stagnate because they do not periodically assess their effectiveness, optimize workflows, or update security policies. Conducting SOC maturity assessments based on frameworks such as MITRE ATT&CK, the NIST Cybersecurity Framework, and the Cyber Kill Chain helps organizations identify gaps, improve detection capabilities, and align SOC functions with best practices.

Failure to secure executive buy-in and budget support can limit a SOC's effectiveness. Many SOCs operate with insufficient funding, outdated tools, and inadequate staffing due to a lack of leadership support. Executives often view cybersecurity as a cost center rather than a strategic priority, making it difficult for SOC teams to secure necessary investments. To avoid this issue, SOC leaders must effectively communicate the value of security operations, present measurable risk reduction metrics, and demonstrate how a well-funded SOC protects business continuity. Aligning SOC objectives with business goals helps justify budget requests and ensures long-term sustainability.

Building a SOC without considering scalability leads to future challenges as the organization grows. A SOC designed for a small IT environment may struggle to handle increased data volumes, expanded networks, and global operations. Organizations must design SOC architectures that support scalability, whether through cloud-based security solutions, decentralized SOC models, or follow-the-sun operations. Implementing flexible security frameworks ensures that SOCs can adapt to new technologies, business expansions, and evolving cyber threats without requiring costly overhauls.

Avoiding these common pitfalls requires a combination of strategic planning, continuous training, process refinement, and the right mix of technology. Organizations that take a holistic approach to SOC development—focusing on people, processes, and technology—are more likely to build an effective, resilient, and scalable security operation capable of defending against modern cyber threats. By proactively addressing these challenges, organizations can ensure that their SOC remains a strong and adaptable component of their overall cybersecurity strategy.

Conclusion: Ensuring Long-Term Success of a SOC

A Security Operations Center (SOC) is not a one-time project or a static entity; it is a continuously evolving function that must adapt to new threats, emerging technologies, and shifting business priorities. Ensuring the long-term success of a SOC requires a commitment to continuous improvement, strategic investment, and alignment with organizational goals. A well-established SOC serves as the backbone of an organization's cybersecurity defense, providing proactive threat detection, rapid incident response, and resilience against cyber threats. To maintain effectiveness, SOCs must focus on key areas such as technology evolution, workforce development, process optimization, and executive support.

One of the critical factors in sustaining a high-performing SOC is the ability to evolve with technological advancements. Cyber threats are constantly changing, and attackers continuously develop new tactics, techniques, and procedures (TTPs) to bypass traditional security measures. A SOC that relies on outdated tools and legacy detection methods will struggle to identify modern threats. Investing in advanced security technologies such as artificial intelligence (AI), machine learning (ML), extended detection and response (XDR), and cloud-native security solutions ensures that the SOC remains capable of handling emerging attack vectors. Regular technology assessments and upgrades help organizations maintain an agile and adaptable SOC that can defend against evolving cyber risks.

Automation and orchestration play a significant role in enhancing SOC efficiency and scalability. As security alert volumes increase, SOC analysts can become overwhelmed by the sheer number of incidents that require investigation. Security Orchestration, Automation, and Response (SOAR) platforms help streamline repetitive tasks such as alert triage, threat intelligence enrichment, and incident containment. By automating routine security operations, SOCs can reduce response times, minimize human error, and allow analysts to focus on high-priority threats. Implementing automated playbooks ensures consistency in incident response and enhances the SOC's ability to mitigate cyber threats effectively.

Workforce development is another essential component of long-term SOC success. The cybersecurity skills gap remains a global challenge, making it difficult for organizations to find and retain skilled SOC analysts. High employee turnover and burnout are common issues in SOC environments due to the high-stress nature of the job. Organizations must prioritize continuous training, career development, and mentorship programs to retain top talent and ensure that SOC teams remain engaged and motivated. Investing in employee well-being, offering professional certifications, and creating clear career progression paths help reduce attrition and build a resilient security workforce.

A successful SOC also requires a strong culture of collaboration and knowledge sharing. Cybersecurity is a team effort, and SOC operations must integrate seamlessly with other business functions, including IT, legal, compliance, and executive leadership. Cross-functional collaboration ensures that security incidents are handled efficiently and that business continuity is maintained during cyber crises. Regular incident response drills, tabletop exercises, and red team assessments help strengthen communication between SOC teams and other departments, improving the overall security posture of the organization.

Threat intelligence integration is another crucial element in maintaining SOC effectiveness. Security teams must stay ahead of adversaries by leveraging real-time threat intelligence feeds, industry-specific threat-sharing platforms, and proactive threat-hunting initiatives. By analyzing emerging attack patterns, indicators of compromise (IOCs), and adversary behaviors, SOC teams can improve detection capabilities and prevent attacks before they cause significant damage. Integrating threat intelligence into Security Information and Event Management (SIEM) systems and security analytics platforms enhances situational awareness and enables proactive defense strategies.

Regulatory compliance and governance play a vital role in ensuring the long-term sustainability of a SOC. Organizations must adhere to industry-specific regulations such as the General Data Protection Regulation (GDPR), the Health Insurance Portability and Accountability Act (HIPAA), and the Payment Card Industry Data Security Standard (PCI DSS). A well-documented SOC governance framework ensures that security policies, incident response procedures, and data protection measures comply with regulatory requirements. Conducting regular security audits, risk assessments, and compliance reviews helps organizations identify gaps, address vulnerabilities, and demonstrate a commitment to cybersecurity best practices.

Metrics and performance measurement are essential for evaluating SOC success and identifying areas for improvement. Key performance indicators (KPIs) such as Mean Time to Detect (MTTD), Mean Time to Respond (MTTR), false positive rates, and security event correlation efficiency provide valuable insights into SOC effectiveness. By continuously monitoring these metrics, organizations can assess their SOC's strengths and weaknesses, make data-driven decisions, and implement necessary improvements. Regular SOC maturity assessments based on frameworks such as the MITRE ATT&CK framework and the NIST Cybersecurity Framework help organizations benchmark their security operations against industry standards.

Executive support and leadership buy-in are crucial for sustaining a SOC's long-term success. Without adequate funding, resources, and strategic direction, SOC teams may struggle to keep up with the growing complexity of cyber threats. SOC leaders must effectively communicate the value of security operations to executive stakeholders, demonstrating how a well-funded SOC contributes to risk reduction, regulatory compliance, and business continuity. Presenting clear metrics, incident case studies, and return-on-investment (ROI) reports helps justify security investments and ensures that SOC initiatives align with overall business objectives.

Scalability and adaptability are key considerations for long-term SOC growth. As organizations expand, acquire new assets, and adopt emerging technologies, SOC operations must scale accordingly. A SOC that is not designed for scalability may struggle to manage increased data volumes, cloud-based infrastructure, and globally distributed environments. Implementing a flexible SOC architecture that supports cloud-native security monitoring, decentralized SOC models, and global threat intelligence sharing ensures that security operations can grow with the organization's needs. A follow-the-sun SOC model, where security teams across different time zones collaborate to provide continuous threat monitoring, enhances global security resilience.

Continuous improvement is the foundation of a successful SOC. Cyber threats will never remain static, and neither should security operations. Organizations must foster a culture of adaptability, encouraging SOC teams to experiment with new threat detection techniques, refine incident response playbooks, and engage in ongoing security research. Regular lessons-learned reviews after security incidents provide valuable insights into what worked well and what needs improvement. SOC teams should actively participate in cybersecurity conferences, industry working groups, and collaborative research initiatives to stay ahead of emerging threats.

The long-term success of a SOC depends on its ability to evolve, innovate, and remain aligned with organizational security objectives. By investing in cutting-edge technology, fostering a skilled workforce, optimizing security processes, and securing executive support, organizations can build a SOC that not only detects and mitigates threats but also serves as a strategic asset for business resilience. Cybersecurity is a continuous journey, and a well-maintained SOC ensures that organizations remain prepared to defend against the evolving cyber threat landscape.